NEW DIRECTIONS FOR PROGRAM EVALUATION
A Publication of the American Evaluation Association

William R. Shadish, *Memphis State University*
EDITOR-IN-CHIEF

Evaluating Chicago School Reform

Richard P. Niemiec
Chicago Public Schools

Herbert J. Walberg
University of Illinois at Chicago

EDITORS

Number 59, Fall 1993

JOSSEY-BASS PUBLISHERS
San Francisco

EVALUATING CHICAGO SCHOOL REFORM
Richard P. Niemiec, Herbert J. Walberg (eds.)
New Directions for Program Evaluation, no. 59
William R. Shadish, Editor-in-Chief

Microfilm copies of issues and articles are available in 16mm and 35mm, as well as microfiche in 105mm, through University Microfilms Inc., 300 North Zeeb Road, Ann Arbor, Michigan 48106.

LC 85-644749   ISSN 0164-7989   ISBN 1-55542-678-6

NEW DIRECTIONS FOR PROGRAM EVALUATION is part of The Jossey-Bass Education Series and is published quarterly by Jossey-Bass Inc., Publishers (publication number USPS 449-050).

EDITORIAL CORRESPONDENCE should be sent to the editor-in-chief, William R. Shadish, Department of Psychology, Memphis State University, Memphis, Tennessee 38152.

10% POST
CONSUMER
WASTE

INSTRUCTIONS TO CONTRIBUTORS

NEW DIRECTIONS FOR PROGRAM EVALUATION (NDPE), a quarterly sourcebook, is an official publication of the American Evaluation Association. As such, NDPE publishes empirical, methodological, and theoretical work on all aspects of program evaluation and related fields. Substantive areas may include any area of social programming such as mental health, education, job training, medicine, or public health, but may also extend the boundaries of evaluation to such topics as product evaluation, personnel evaluation, policy analysis, or technology assessment. In all cases, the focus on evaluation is more important than the particular substantive topic.

NDPE does not consider or publish unsolicited single manuscripts. Each issue of NDPE is devoted to a single topic, with contributions solicited, organized, reviewed, and edited by a guest editor. Issues may take any of several forms, such as a series of related chapters, a monograph, or a long article followed by brief critical commentaries. In all cases, proposals must follow a specific format, which can be obtained from the editor-in-chief. These proposals are sent to members of the editorial board, and to relevant substantive experts, for peer review. This process may result in rejection, acceptance, or a recommendation to revise and resubmit. However, NDPE is committed to working constructively with potential guest editors to help them develop acceptable proposals. Close contact with the editor-in-chief is encouraged during proposal preparation and generation.

COPIES OF NDPE's "Guide for Proposal Development" and "Proposal Format" can be obtained from the editor-in-chief:

William R. Shadish, Editor-in-Chief
New Directions for Program Evaluation
Department of Psychology
Memphis State University
Memphis, TN 38152
Office: 901-678-4687
FAX: 901-678-2579
Bitnet: SHADISHWR@MEMSTVX1

CONTENTS

EDITORS' NOTES

It has been called "the most radical educational experiment in the United States." Since 1989, the Chicago Public School (CPS) System has been undergoing a major restructuring that has shifted responsibility for running schools from central board and staff to local school councils composed mainly of laypeople. The experiment involves over 550 schools, 410,000 students, and 25,000 teachers and support staff. It is the most thorough transition of power to local schools among major cities in the United States. This volume, *Evaluating Chicago School Reform*, brings together a diverse group of authors with multiple perspectives to examine the reform effort.

In 1987, the U.S. Secretary of Education William Bennett declared that CPSs were "the worst in the nation." There was no denying that the schools were in bad shape. By almost any measure of school effectiveness, CPSs were doing a poor job of educating children. Student scores on standardized tests were dismal. Only 3 percent of the high schools, for example, scored above the national average in reading in 1982. In mathematics only 7 percent scored above the national average. In suburban Cook County, surrounding Chicago, every high school reported scores above the national average.

The comparisons were equally dismal for college entrance examinations and student dropout rates. The national average for the American College Test (a widely used college entrance examination) in 1982 was 18.8 (19.1 in Illinois). The average CPS student scored 13, or approximately 30 percentile points below the national average. In addition, approximately 50 percent of all students who entered CPSs dropped out.

Perhaps the most damning indictment of CPSs in the 1980s was the fact that almost half of the CPS teachers sent their own children to private schools. When those who knew the system best chose costly alternatives to a free service, there clearly was something very wrong with the system. The situation was analogous to roughly five out of every ten American automobile workers choosing Toyotas or Hondas rather than their own companies' products.

In addition, central office personnel were numerous and had ill-defined and often overlapping jobs descriptions. There were approximately thirty-three hundred bureaucrats performing a variety of administrative tasks, but their numbers did not seem to reflect their service to the students or teachers. Between 1976 and 1986, for example, the number of CPS students fell by 18 percent, yet the number of central office and district personnel increased by 30 percent. This increase did not reflect the number of support staff, clerks, and lunchroom workers. These were administrators and support service personnel.

NEW DIRECTIONS FOR PROGRAM EVALUATION, no. 59, Fall 1993   © Jossey-Bass Publishers

The Illinois General Assembly adopted the Chicago School Reform Act of 1988 (P.A. 85-1418) to improve the quality of education and achievement in Chicago. This reform effort is the most far-reaching and drastic educational change in any big city school system in recent decades within the United States. Power shifted from a heavily centralized bureaucracy to local school councils (LSCs), each composed of eleven members: the principal, two teachers, six parents, and two community members. LSCs have considerable control over school budgets and the power to hire and dismiss principals and teachers. They set policy for students and teachers and formulate plans for school improvement. In some cases, LSCs have fired longtime principals, mandated more emphasis on core curriculum, and set uniform dress codes.

The Chicago School Reform Act and its effects are described in greater detail in Chapter One. Stephen K. Clements and Oliver A. Kimberly examine the events that preceded the reform movement and discuss political and evaluation issues.

Penny A. Sebring and Anthony S. Bryk, in Chapter Two, describe the organization and work of the Consortium on Chicago School Research, a group of universities, reform groups, and staff of the Illinois Department of Education that received substantial long-term funding to plan, execute, and report on evaluations of CPSs. The consortium employed an unusual and extensive process to identify indicators of reform and organize ongoing evaluations, and the group carried out an extensive survey of CPS teachers, principals, and LSC members, the results of which were reported not only for the system as a whole but also on a customized basis for each of the hundreds of schools participating in the survey.

In Chapter Three, John Q. Easton and Albert L. Bennett report on two major surveys of eighteen thousand teachers and five hundred school principals. The results of the surveys indicate that, despite initial misgivings, both teachers and principals think that the reform effort is proceeding reasonably well.

In Chapter Four, G. Alfred Hess, Jr., Susan Leigh Flinspach, and Susan P. Ryan report on intensive, longitudinal case studies of fourteen CPSs. As this research revealed, many of the changes that were envisioned are not actually taking place at the school level. The authors use an anthropological perspective to identify the internal and external barriers to reform and recommend policies and practices to overcome them.

In Chapter Five, Thomas Hehir describes the restructuring of special education services and practices made possible by the reform movement in Chicago. This change was particularly important because there are forty-four thousand special education students in CPSs. In addition, there were numerous complaints to the U.S. Office of Civil Rights and subsequent consent decrees concerning classification and treatment of special needs students. Hehir examines the effects of departmental changes, and the greater accessibility of educational opportunities for special needs students brought about by reform. He also illustrates how the reform affected one particular department and how the reform mandate was carried out and evaluated.

In Chapter Six, James G. Cibulka offers a political science perspective on four Chicago high schools, using interviews with and observations of such stakeholders as teachers, students, parents, and administrators. He stresses the governing role of the LSCs as balanced against other sources of power. He also compares and contrasts the governance roles of CPSs and Chicago Catholic high schools.

In Chapter Seven, Melanie F. Sikorski, Trudy Wallace, Winifred E. Stariha, and Vivian E. Rankin examine the effects of school programs that have been implemented or substantially modified during the course of the decentralization effort. Four programs—the Coalition of Essential Schools, the Paideia Program, the Algebra Project, and the Home and Hospital programs—are described and the results of their evaluations presented.

In Chapter Eight, three prominent Chicagoans—Asish Sen, Jacqueline B. Vaughn, and Thomas Flanagan—provide short perspectives on the current workings and the future of Chicago school reform. Finally, in Chapter Nine, we summarize the apparent effects of school reform in terms of such indicators of educational excellence as student achievement, attendance, and dropout rates, and parental and community satisfaction.

The views and opinions expressed in this volume are attributable solely to the authors and no official endorsements are made. The second editor gratefully acknowledges the support of the University of Illinois Center for Urban Educational Research and Development and the Temple University Center for Education in the Inner Cities sponsored by the United States Department of Education.

Richard P. Niemiec
Herbert J. Walberg
Editors

RICHARD P. NIEMIEC *teaches in the Chicago public schools.*

HERBERT J. WALBERG *is research professor of education at the University of Illinois at Chicago.*

This chapter provides an introduction to and describes the background of the Chicago School Reform Act.

School Reform in Chicago: An Overview

Stephen K. Clements, Oliver A. Kimberly

Chicago's school reform effort is a mammoth undertaking that began in earnest four years ago. Numerous individuals and organizations have attempted to assess this effort, and nearly every methodological approach has been employed in scrutinizing school life under reform. The general consensus so far is that reform is moving the school system in the right direction, though slowly, and there is growing concern that institutional forces of one sort or another could soon bring progress to a halt. In this chapter, we provide a retrospective on the first few years of reform in an attempt to illuminate the reform effort's progress, identify its shortcomings, and provide a context for interpreting events to come. Our comments are based on a review of the media's coverage of reform, information gained through fieldwork in Chicago, various published reports and studies of reform, and interviews with an array of individuals involved in school reform.

Reform Plan: A Thumbnail Sketch

The Chicago School Reform Act of 1988 mandated that student achievement levels in Chicago schools meet the national average within five years. To reach that goal, the act sought to shift as much control as possible from the system's central office to Chicago's public schools. Reform activists and legislators who shaped the measure opted against familiar site-based management models that use teams of teachers and administrators as decision makers. Instead, they devised a grass-roots scheme that involves participatory site management teams called local school councils (LSCs), one for each school, aimed at placing school management in the hands of parents, whose children have the greatest stake in the schools' well-being. Biannual plebiscites allow each community to choose six parents and two community representatives to serve on a school's LSC. They are joined by two teachers and the school's principal, for a total of eleven members.

LSCs are equipped with various powers and responsibilities. Each LSC, rather than system bureaucrats or city politicians, is responsible for hiring a principal for its school and employing him or her on a four-year contract. Each LSC also decides how to spend its school's portion of state Chapter I compensatory funds. Many of these funds had hitherto been diverted by system bureaucrats away from school sites to shore up the central system's general overhead and budget. By phasing out that diversion over five years, the reform act provided LSCs with a greater degree of fiscal authority. In addition, reform measures have developed various mechanisms for communication and coordination among LSCs.

The reform act was a product of considerable political wrangling. As such, the legislation is replete with compromises and ambiguities. It may take years to settle some issues of power and control that have arisen during implementation.

The framework of the 1988 reform act has been phased in over the past three years and is for the most part up and running. The first LSC election was held in late 1989, when seventeen thousand candidates vied for nearly six thousand two-year positions. The second LSC election, held in autumn 1991, was far less competitive; only eighty-two hundred candidates ran. Clearly, the word is out that running a school is hard and sobering work. (Chicagoans' eagerness to serve on LSCs may be dampened further by a federal court's decision to hold four LSC members personally liable for firing a principal.)

The new LSCs have met regularly since the first election. All of them have had to draft and periodically update school improvement plans for their sites. Many have had to decide on issues of curriculum and staff usage. And all have had either to reappoint their incumbent principals or to choose new ones to lead their schools through reform. (By the end of the reform's third year, 40 percent of all principals were "new" to the system, meaning they had not served as a Chicago principal prior to reform.) LSCs have also had to decide how to spend their schools' discretionary accounts, which have grown with the reform's shift of Chapter I funds to school sites. Ironically, LSCs have utilized this money—on average, the shift gives each LSC about $340,000 per year—to grow their own minibureaucracies. At last count, LSCs had hired fifty-four hundred additional staffers since reform began, including counselors, teachers, assistant principals, and teacher aides.

Presiding over reform implementation has been General Superintendent Ted Kimbrough, formerly an administrator in Compton, California. The reform act authorized a search for a new superintendent, and

Kimbrough was the choice of the 1989–90 Chicago Board of Education (a five-member interim team appointed by Mayor Richard M. Daley). Kimbrough has had an embattled tenure, especially during 1992, as he has attempted to cope with central office staff cuts and the chronic budget problems of the Chicago Public School System. Not long after he began the last year of his three-year contract, he announced that he would not seek another term as superintendent. In January 1993, the Board of Education bought out the remainder of his contract.

Assessments of Reform Progress

Structural features of school governance have changed throughout the school system. To varying degrees, LSCs have brought greater accountability and parental involvement to virtually every school. As noted earlier, there is sentiment in the city that Chicago's reform represents a significant step forward and has directed the school system toward long-term systemic improvement.

But reform experiences have differed vastly from school to school, making it difficult to gauge the reform's systemwide effects. Some schools have shifted course dramatically, their LSCs and recently installed (or newly energized) principals offering welcome leadership and vision to the school communities. With a legislative mandate for strong parental involvement and extra funds to supplement staff and programs, some schools have made real strides in moving student achievement levels toward state and national averages. Others, particularly many magnet schools, already were accustomed to strong front office leadership and active parental involvement. With prereform student achievement at decent levels, such schools tend to perceive scant need to make significant changes. Still other schools receive few additional compensatory education dollars for LSC discretionary use, diminishing their LSCs' capacity to make changes. And some schools simply do not have the will or capacity to change at this point. In all, estimates one student of Chicago reform, structural change appears to have had but a marginal impact on learning environments and test scores in fully half of Chicago's schools.

The North Central Regional Educational Laboratory recently completed its own extensive survey of reform and concluded that most reform-driven changes have heretofore not focused on curriculum or instruction. Rather, reform has primarily altered the structures of school governance to allow for greater school site decision making. Unfortunately, many school-level practitioners might not be hungry for additional authority. A Chicago-area education consultant found in the report "little indication" that teachers and local administrators had assumed greater levels of responsibility for student achievement. "Clearly," he wrote, "schools know and understand that they are responsible for teaching students; they do not, however, accept accountability."

While early reform measures may not provide an immediate boost in test scores, student achievement remains the best measure of the reform's impact, and improved achievement is the reform's explicit goal. Given the reform's scant success in reducing the city's dropout rate, stagnant test scores are especially worrisome. Whether and when reform initiatives reported by principals, teachers, and other students of Chicago schooling will have an impact on test scores is unclear, but good news in the form of achievement must come before Chicago-style reform can be branded a success.

School Reform and Barriers to Change

These early assessments of reform demonstrate the difficulty of systematically altering the behavior and attitudes of thousands of individuals operating in a highly structured, enormously regulated, and still largely centralized school system. Indeed, to many observers, the way of doing school business in the United States—as practiced by teachers, local and central administrators, politicians, and school boards—simply has not changed significantly in a large enough number of schools to transform the schooling process. The Chicago Public School System remains a highly centralized and bureaucratic operation, and LSCs are limited in their ability to alter the status quo. As noted, LSCs can exercise control over the principalship, certain discretionary funds, curriculum (to some extent), and sundry other aspects of school policy, but the bulk of school budget decisions remains in the hands of the superintendent and numerous central office administrators, all of whom continue to operate largely by formula. Purchases still must be made through the central office, and that office dictates the amount and timing of the bountiful paperwork that teachers and administrators complete. Moreover, the superintendent has not been keen to relinquish power; his actions and words have portended little devolution of authority, reflecting limited commitment to Chicago-style reform.

As a result, many in Chicago's education trenches continue to perceive the central office as a barrier to reform, an organization inclined to stifle promising practices that arise at creative schools. Nor has the Chicago Board of Education been a well-organized catalyst for decentralization. The reform act created the School Board Nominating Commission, composed largely of LSC members and a few mayoral appointees, to recruit and screen board candidates. The point, of course, was to link the board selection process to LSCs, the basic units of reform, while minimizing political interference. Unfortunately, the resulting fifteen-member board has spent much of the past two years immersed in disputes about reform implementation and budget reductions rather than nudging the bureaucracy toward further decentralization. The board also remains bound by massive citywide collective bargaining agreements with twenty-two employee unions. Those agreements virtually dictate how teachers and other school staff spend their time. And while LSCs can get waivers from the Chicago Teachers Union if they want to tinker with teaching schedules or duties, few have sought to do so.

Chicago's general political environment has also been a hindrance to effective reform. The state government in Springfield seems disinclined to clarify ambiguous portions of the reform legislation, preferring instead to let the city work through implementation problems on its own. The state government also faces a several-years-long fiscal crisis and has been unable to provide extra funding for reform. Even the mayor's support for reform has been languid. He has demonstrated concern for the school system's fiscal condition but has not weighed in on other key education issues. Most of the city's aldermen and alderwomen have avoided the school reform issue, sensing that ties to the ailing education system could burn them politically.

The city will also likely continue to face fiscal problems with the school system. State and city revenues for education have grown slowly during the past few years, and the reform act, though revenue-neutral, in effect depleted city coffers when it began shifting Chapter I funds to school sites. Between the shift in Chapter I funds and slow growth, the school system's budget has been severely strapped during the reform's early years. The board and mayor managed, only through clever accounting practices, to shore up projected deficits and open schools in September 1992 without a teachers' strike. But next year's deficit is projected to be so large—now estimated at around $300 million (out of a $2.5 billion overall budget)— that a fiscal shell game may not succeed. The picture is more grim for succeeding years: A business-sponsored study released last spring estimated that the system faces deficits as high as $540 million in 1996 and $515 million in 1997. As noted earlier, the legislature in Springfield has been unwilling to offer Chicago relief, and it is unclear how the city and state will resolve these fiscal problems.

Over the past year, these varied—and gridlocked—forces have essentially paralyzed the school system in a state of partial centralization, and those forces remain intact during this fourth year of reform. Most schools are in fact structurally equipped to assume greater authority and accountability for improved student achievement. Their ability to exercise that authority, however, still depends on a central office and political process well beyond their control.

Future of Reform

To translate reform from structural change into substantial gains in student achievement, schools will need no less than visionary leadership, imaginative teachers, energetic LSC members, and an organized, responsive community. They will also need to realize substantial autonomy, which is at the root of Chicago's reform design. The reform act planted seeds for change, but whether those seeds will be watered, fertilized, given sunlight, and otherwise allowed to grow depends on the interaction among local communities and the key personalities and components of Chicago's education system. The mayor, for example, will continue to be a key player in the reform. He clearly does not want to offend the Chicago Teachers Union, which still thinks and acts like a large, special interest organization. But he has pressured the Chicago Board of Education to be responsible about its fiscal and educational decisions, and he seems willing to support further decentralization efforts.

The school board could also move the system toward further decentralization and more meaningful changes in the education process. For the near term, at least, these steps are unlikely given the unwieldy size of the board and the disparate ideas held by board members. In addition, the board in upcoming months will be choosing a new superintendent to oversee the future of the reform effort. Given the political dynamics in the city and on the board, it is possible that the Chicago Public School System will again be run by an executive with strong centralizing instincts. Loosely organized groups of LSC members could increasingly influence the system. One such assemblage of about one hundred LSC members, in summer 1992, proffered a plan for Chicago's public schools to operate autonomously within three years. Under the plan, all but $15 million of the $91 million in annual funds spent on the system's central administration would be redistributed among schools, and LSCs would be allowed to hire teachers and control a wide variety of budget areas, including in-service training, curriculum development, performance assessment, and facility maintenance. As expected, this radical plan was dismissed by the Chicago Teachers Union and the superintendent. But the idea of complete control over schooling will not die soon, and the cause might soon be taken up by other groups.

Three years into an ambitious effort, then, it is clear that many Chicagoans are pleased with the basic structure and general direction of reform. Most acknowledge that important education issues have not yet been adequately addressed, but the mechanisms appear in place to begin moving beyond concerns of governance and into the teaching and learning process. Even in a cash-strapped system, some money is available to many LSCs to help them make selective improvements. The business community maintains its interest in education and continues to fund a major reform group and to sponsor periodic studies of the system. Philanthropic money flows into city schools from many local foundations and other donors. And LSCs have garnered considerable local interest, reflecting widespread approval for reform's participatory principles.

However notable, these points are secondary to the ultimate objective of the reform effort: substantial improvement in student achievement. So far, test scores systemwide have been relatively unaffected by reform. We believe that the transformation Chicago seeks for its public schools will not come, and scores will not substantially improve, until authority devolves further from the central office and the logic of the LSC-based reform act is allowed to manifest itself freely in every school across the city.

STEPHEN K. CLEMENTS, formerly associate director of the Educational Excellence Network, is currently a graduate student in political science at the University of Chicago.

OLIVER A. KIMBERLY is a research analyst at the Educational Excellence Network, a project of the Hudson Institute in Indianapolis, Indiana.

The Consortium on Chicago School Research is a unique research enterprise that is attempting to achieve a productive blend of rigorous social science and vital democratic activities. So far, it has facilitated the development of a research agenda on Chicago school reform and completed surveys of teachers and principals.

Charting Reform in Chicago Schools: Pluralistic Policy Research

Penny A. Sebring, Anthony S. Bryk

In 1990, a dozen Chicago-area organizations formed the Consortium on Chicago School Research to undertake a range of research activities designed to assist the implementation of school reform, assess its progress, and, in general, support school improvement in the city. The consortium seeks to encourage (1) broad access to the process of setting the research agenda, (2) collection and regular reporting of systematic information on the condition of education in the city, (3) high standards of quality in research design, data collection, and analysis, and (4) wide dissemination and discussion of research findings.

As a research enterprise, the consortium is unusual. It is deliberately multipartisan; members include faculty from area universities, research staff from the Chicago public schools, representatives of the Illinois State Board of Education and the North Central Regional Educational Laboratory (NCREL), researchers in advocacy groups, as well as other interested individuals and organizations. The consortium is funded through multiple sources and accomplishes much of its work through in-kind contributions of member organizations. Although located at a university, the consortium maintains considerable independence and is not tied to any particular institution.

In this chapter, we describe the consortium's approach to pluralistic policy research and the historical and theoretical roots of these efforts. In addition, we discuss the organization of the consortium, how it functions, what it is trying to accomplish, and the initial benefits and shortcomings of its approach.

New Directions for Program Evaluation, no. 59, Fall 1993 © Jossey-Bass Publishers

Chicago: The Context

Assessing school reform in Chicago is a daunting prospect. The Chicago School Reform Act of 1988 realigned power and authority relationships. Parents and community members gained influence; principals lost tenure but gained more control over their schools; the central and district offices were slashed but the personnel still expected to play a new role, supporting rather than directing local schools. Furthermore, significant decisions affecting the reform take place beyond the school system. The legislature, the governor, the mayor, and the School Finance Authority all have considerable authority over policy and finances. Clearly, there are multiple sites of decision making and policy responsibility that must be taken into account. All of these groups need ongoing high-quality information about the progress of school reform and school improvement.

In addition, there are thousands of school constituents: students, parents, teachers, principals, administrators, other school personnel, local school council members, the business community, and the public. Reform has also catalyzed considerable activity among advocacy groups, community agencies, foundations, businesses, universities, and professional organizations to provide assistance to schools and participate in networks and partnerships. These constituents and groups all have a significant stake in school improvement.

The political and social context of school reform in Chicago demands a pluralistic approach to policy research. The consortium seeks to bring these diverse stakeholders into the process of shaping the information that is to be collected and reported. In this way, interest groups participate in building information bases that they can use to argue their cases. Pluralistic policy research furnishes an information base for policy development in a context where multiple parties compete, negotiate, and otherwise participate in policy development with equal access to relevant and credible information.

Theoretical Underpinnings of Pluralistic Policy Research: Dewey's Notions of Informed Public Opinion

Writing some sixty-five years ago, John Dewey (1927), in *The Public and Its Problems,* pointed to the critical role of social science knowledge and expertise in strengthening America's democratic institutions. Democracy relies on informed public opinion, and in order to develop intelligent public opinion, the public needs to understand the consequences and ramifications of society's collective policies, actions, and institutional policies, actions, and institutional arrangements. Dewey argued that one of the great problems for democracy was the lack of data for making good judgments. He placed responsibility for bridging this gap directly on social science experts.

Dewey cautioned, however, that social scientists cannot practice their craft in isolation. If knowledge is a precondition of informed public judgment, then inquiry must proceed in close proximity to contemporary events. Public policy uninformed by knowledge is collective ignorance, and research disconnected from the public and its concerns is sterile and useless.

According to Dewey (1927, p. 176), broad dissemination of knowledge is critical: "A thing is fully known only when it is published, shared, socially accessible." He likened the task of disseminating knowledge to sowing seeds in a field. Information needs to be shared in such a way that it can take root and have a chance to grow. Dewey recalled Tocqueville's observation about democracy. In comparison to other forms of government, democratic government must be educative; it requires people to openly discuss and clarify their common interests. Dewey noted that for the full effect of social intelligence to be felt, new knowledge must travel by word of mouth in local communities where it can be incorporated into the democratic process.

Dewey's advice directly addressed a fundamental issue in modern democratic society. Society's continued progress makes increasing demands on technical expertise. If modern society is to remain vital, however, and not dissolve into a technical aristocracy with a large uninvolved public (see, for example, Barber's [1984] critique of thin democracy), then this knowledge must be broadly held. The creation of structures and institutions to effect such learning and participation is even more important today than it was during Dewey's time.

Stakeholder-Based Evaluation and Pluralistic Policy Analysis

Although Dewey emphasized the need to integrate research knowledge into public debate, evaluation theorists in the 1960s and 1970s tended to focus their attention on the information needs of policymakers and program managers. As concern grew about the lack of use of these studies, evaluators (Patton, 1978; Stake, 1980; Weiss, 1972) began to attend to a broad group of stakeholders, people who were affected in one way or another by the operation of a program. If evaluators could consult with various stakeholders before undertaking their projects, it was argued, evaluations would be more relevant, and policymakers and stakeholders would be more likely to use the results.

Some theorists also claimed that evaluators were morally obligated to provide an opportunity for stakeholders in a program to influence the design of the evaluation (House, 1980; Stake, 1980; Weiss, 1983). Weiss (1983), for example, wrote that, if an agency commissions a study, it has the power to determine the questions that will be asked and, ultimately, the information that will emerge and undergo scrutiny. The needs and priorities of the agency will prevail, but little attention will be paid to those of the clients (see Guba and Lincoln, 1989).

Weiss recognized that programs have multiple stakeholders who have different interests and who will want to ask different questions. Similarly, at the point when results become available, Weiss noted that there may be competition among these stakeholders regarding their interpretations. The evaluation could become "mired in a morass of conflicting expectations" (Weiss, 1972, p. 6). (The Consortium on Chicago School Research expects such competition and actually encourages it. During early phases of a study, we consult broadly with stakeholders to develop the purposes and content of the investigation. As we move to the release of findings, briefings are held with various groups before the write-up of the final study report. Even after a report is complete, individuals can submit and publicize alternative explanations. We believe that better policy is likely to emerge from such a competition of ideas.)

Weiss and Bucuvalas's (1980) study of policymakers' use of social science research considerably clarified the impact of this kind of research on policy. They found that policymakers mainly used research information to enlighten themselves or to help them understand the bigger picture. They were much less likely to use data instrumentally, that is, to make discrete decisions.

> As the decision makers whom we interviewed reported, a much more common mode of research use is the diffuse and undirected infiltration of research ideas into their understanding of the world. They reported few deliberate and targeted uses of the findings from individual studies. Rather, they absorbed the concepts and generalizations from many studies over extended periods of time and they integrated research ideas, along with other information, into their interpretation of events. . . . The research information and ideas that percolate into their stock of knowledge represent a part of the intellectual capital upon which they draw in the regular course of their work [1980, p. 263].

Enlightenment does not solve immediate problems or give answers to specific questions. Instead, it arms men and women with concepts and evidence that help them search for solutions.

Stake is one of the most ardent proponents of stakeholder-based evaluation (Shadish, Cook, and Leviton, 1991). He believes that evaluation should help local stakeholders determine the changes that they want to implement. The evaluation is an emerging process that unfolds primarily from the ideas and questions of program managers and others who have a stake in the program. Stake eventually dubbed this approach "responsive evaluation." The advantages of responsive evaluation are that important program variables emerge from the discussions with stakeholders, change efforts by local stakeholders are encouraged, and local control is increased. Stake asserted that there is no single value system driving an evaluation. Rather, "the evaluation encounters a pluralism of values" (Shadish, Cook, and Leviton, 1991, p. 274; see also Guba and Lincoln, 1989).

The first attempts to put stakeholder-based evaluation into practice occurred in 1977, when the National Institute of Education (NIE) commissioned evaluations of Cities-in-Schools and Operation Push\Excel. The request for proposals carried instructions to evaluators regarding the need to be responsive to various local groups (Bryk, 1983).

To assess the utility of this approach, NIE asked the Huron Institute and the Center for Instructional Research and Curriculum Evaluation at the University of Illinois to collaborate on a study of the stakeholder experience. These researchers found that, for various reasons, the stakeholder approach had not been fully implemented in either case. The Cities-in-Schools evaluator worked more with decision makers than with stakeholders. The Push\Excel evaluation was beset by many other issues that tended to overshadow the stakeholder practices. Nevertheless, analysis of these two evaluations illuminated the difficulty of attempting to produce generalizable social science information while at the same time attending to the questions and needs of local stakeholders (Bryk, 1983).

In 1979, two years after these evaluations began, James Coleman and his colleagues at the University of Chicago launched an investigation of stakeholders' information needs in preparation for designing the High School and Beyond Survey, a federally funded longitudinal study of high school seniors and sophomores (Coleman, Bartot, Lewin-Epstein, and Olson, 1979). These researchers engaged in an extensive process of consultation with policymakers and various education interest groups.

Like Weiss, the authors discarded the notion that policy research should simply advise the government or those who are in power. Instead, they argued that policy formation emerges from a pluralistic process where various interests compete with one another in determining policy. The role of policy research is to inform not just the policymaker or government body but also the many interest groups, so that they can press their cases on the basis of legitimate information.

Based on this perspective, Coleman, Bartot, Lewin-Epstein, and Olson (1979, p. 7) asserted that "at two points in the research, design and dissemination, the research should be greatly affected by interests, broad and narrow, private and public." They cautioned, however, that the information needs of separate interest groups should not be the sole determinant of the research design. The research investigator, who is knowledgeable of the area under discussion, provides coherence and overall structure to the research design. "The design should be *responsive* to a variety of interests, but should be *responsible* to none" (pp. 11–12). Hence, the task of designing the research involves analysis of the policy-making process, identification of interest groups and policies for which the research is relevant, and determination of the kinds of information that are relevant to interest groups and policymakers. The theoretical task for the researcher is to integrate this knowledge into an overall research design.

Finally, Coleman, Bartot, Lewin-Epstein, and Olson (1979) argued that, at the end of a study, findings must be made available to all parties, not just the government agency. The authors recognized, however, that different interest groups have different capacities to use information: Some have sophisticated research staffs whereas others have very little capability. These differences, too, pose a problem. If the competition among ideas is to be vital and fair, efforts must be made to ensure access not only to the data but also to the necessary technical expertise to understand, ask questions about, and use the data.

Guba and Lincoln (1989) have made the strongest case yet for attending to stakeholders. Like Stake, they have argued that stakeholders should have paramount influence on the kind of information collected. They have also called for an expanded role for the evaluator—moving beyond the information gathering to participation in the negotiation process and the identification of action steps.

Fourth-generation evaluation, as outlined by Guba and Lincoln (1989), involves four main phases. First, the evaluation is focused through interaction and negotiation among the various stakeholder groups. Each stakeholder group advances its claims, concerns, and issues. Second, stakeholders confront one another's constructions (understandings) of the phenomena under consideration. When there is agreement, these issues are no longer discussed. Where there is disagreement, stakeholders identify the information that is needed to settle the conflict. Third, information is collected. Fourth, stakeholders come together for negotiation. The evaluator prepares an agenda and helps stakeholders examine the evidence and reach final conclusions regarding the claims, concerns, and issues with which they began. In this final phase, also, the evaluator helps to determine an agenda for action.

In reviewing much of the work on stakeholder-based evaluation, however, Shadish, Cook, and Leviton (1991) cautioned that overreliance on stakeholders' interests may diminish the goal of social problem solving. This perspective was also expressed by Coleman, Bartot, Lewin-Epstein, and Olson (1979). If research is based on a collection of stakeholders' self-interests, there is no guarantee that the research will focus on larger issues that need to be addressed in order to improve programs. It is our contention that researchers play a critical role in keeping research centered on these larger questions. This is the investigators' stake in policy research.

Fundamental Convictions

The work of the Consortium on Chicago School Research is grounded in a new vision about how information and research can help us understand and improve the education enterprise. First, credible social science evidence needs to brought into the public arena so that public debate can be informed, and good judgments can be made. In this regard, researchers must work closely with policymakers, practitioners, and other stakeholders to produce results that are relevant to current problems and issues.

Second, a responsive research agenda must address the issues of multiple audiences. Under Chicago school reform, important decision making now occurs in individual school communities. This means that the needs of principals, teachers, parents, and involved community members must also be addressed. Information is also needed for the system as a whole. More broadly, the research is intended to promote informed public opinion among the citizens of Chicago.

Third, although the research should emanate from stakeholders' concerns, it should not be limited to issues of narrow, short-term self-interest. It must capture the enduring and larger educational concerns. For example, while we want to explore the specific workings of the new governance structure in Chicago, we do not want to lose sight of teaching and classroom practices and their impact on student learning.

Fourth, research rarely provides discrete solutions to problems. Rather, good studies help us to better understand issues and stimulate new ideas. Historically, research has been seen as a specialized tool to be used by public officials to exercise control over schools. Yet research can play a broader role in helping multiple groups identify concerns, gain new concepts for discussing these problems, and use empirical evidence to enlighten such discussions, all of which implies that a key function of research is community education.

Fifth, a responsive research agenda must focus on student outcomes as well as shed light on the processes and institutional arrangements that contribute to these outcomes. This is related to the previous point. While there is a need to monitor "the bottom line," student achievement, we must also examine and understand the factors that contribute to this learning.

Sixth, the research on Chicago school reform should not be a single big study. Rather, it calls for multiple investigators and investigations, involving diverse methodologies and expertise. Some issues call for surveys and complex analyses. Other issues demand in-depth studies by participant observers. Still others call for new forms of collaboration among educators, parents, and researchers. The consortium affords numerous opportunities to engage diverse members of the research community in the city.

Seventh, effective presentation of results and broad dissemination are critical. If research is to serve an educative function, then results must be presented in attractive and simple formats that make liberal use of visual displays and media.

Eighth, research on Chicago schools must respond to immediate needs, but it must also anticipate questions on the horizon. The lack of timeliness of much research is a frequent lament. In fairness, good research is a slow and difficult process. If we are to have more informed policy-making over the long term, then we must create an infrastructure now to address not only today's questions but also those that are likely to arise tomorrow and beyond.

Developing the Research Agenda

One of the initial activities of the consortium was to develop a research agenda to guide the consortium's work as well as that of member organizations involved in research on schools. The process of developing the research agenda was also intended to engage a wide variety of groups and individuals and to begin to build awareness and support of the consortium's work.

Setting of the research agenda is not strictly a scientific matter. Because what gets investigated and reported influences public discussion, it is also a political endeavor. The consortium's research agenda developed out of an extensive consultation process involving a diverse group of individuals and organizations. In seeking this advice, we deliberately cast a wide net, asking Chicagoans about their current experiences with school reform and the issues that they thought might be on the horizon two or three years down the line. In the course of these conversations, we focused both on the improvement of individual schools and on issues affecting the system as a whole.

Individual interviews were conducted with key public officials in the Chicago public schools and in city and state government. More than one hundred individuals also participated in focus groups, including students, parents, teachers, principals, local school council members, subdistrict superintendents, and business leaders. Over fifty civic and community organizations were invited to submit position statements. Toward the end of this process, the consortium convened a conference of educational researchers from around the city, bringing them together with nationally recognized experts on urban schooling to help integrate the stakeholder commentary and add their own insights.

In producing the final research agenda (Bryk and Sebring, 1991), we attempted to synthesize disparate individual expressions, looking for deeper, more fundamental concerns that were broadly shared in order to find the main ideas running throughout the stakeholder commentary. In this process, we paid close attention to the different voices present in Chicago. We listened also to national discussions about efforts to restructure schooling. The agenda is organized around a set of key concerns within four major topic areas. Each concern identified in the major topical areas passed a critical analytical test: Each represents an essential strand in the reweaving of a responsive urban school system.

School Governance. Reform grew out of disillusionment with an unresponsive system that was ineffective in dealing with persistent problems such as declining student performance and teachers' strikes. It was widely argued that a fundamental change was needed to regenerate a sense of agency and commitment. The central instrument chosen to spur such reform was a change in local school governance. This area of the agenda considers issues such as the implementation of local school councils, their decision-making activity, and the politics of school communities. Key concerns are

- New roles and norms for exercising local authority in schools
- Elements of effectively functioning local school councils
- Balancing of authority and responsibility between local schools and the central administration
- Changing role of principals with new responsibilities and increased demands
- Effective participation of parents and communities in school affairs
- Local politics as it contributes to school improvement or impedes change

Teaching and Learning. Governance reform was intended to renew human commitment, foster social cooperation around the schools, and open up new possibilities for school improvement. This area focuses on the ultimate standpoint for judging reform: Does it make a difference in teaching and student learning? Teaching and learning also considers outcomes for students and the key education processes that can advance them:

- Analysis of student performance, attitudes, and aspirations
- Curriculum offerings, opportunities to learn, and students' educational experiences
- Schools' responses to student diversity
- Instructional reform and the professional development of teachers
- School readiness and early childhood services
- Transition to the workplace and to higher education

Quality of Schools as Organizations. If we are to enhance teaching and student learning, we must attend to the organizational conditions that encourage students and teachers to commit effort to their work. The quality of the human interactions that occur within schools is a central concern. This topic area maps out key aspects of the character of schools as institutions that are responsive to their local communities:

- Clarity of mission, a press toward academic work, and a caring, safe environment
- Recruitment of qualified teachers and improvement of classroom practice
- Working conditions for students and teachers that promote respect and personal engagement
- A cooperative ethic with teacher participation in school management
- Strengthening of ties between schools and community institutions
- Enhancement of parental involvement in their children's education

Systemic Issues. Even in a decentralized school system, critical functions still occur at the system level that can either facilitate or constrain local action. This topic area considers the structural and cultural changes required at the system level if school reform is to be institutionalized. Also, key questions about school reform can only be addressed at this level, for example, "Are education opportunities becoming more equitably distributed across the city?" The main concerns in this area are

- Important central functions: providing information, stimulating innovation, and intervening in failing schools
- New norms and working relationships for the Central Service Center and subdistrict staff
- Constraints on the system from federal and state regulations and collective bargaining agreements
- Strengthening of the system's capacity to analyze operations and evaluate programs
- Cumulative effects of local action on education equity across the system

The research agenda also outlined a strategy and cycle for regular reporting. As noted earlier, the consortium seeks to share information broadly, to promote dialogue on school reform and improvement, and to inform these conversations with the best information attainable. In its early work, the consortium has been releasing reports based on single studies. With the full implementation of the consortium structure, we envision the production of two kinds of reports: a Conditions of Education in Chicago series and integrative reports on the development of school reform.

The Conditions of Education reports will be published twice a year and will cycle through the four conceptual areas, so that each area is covered once over a two-year period. These reports are intended to integrate extant information from a variety of sources with new data collected by the consortium. They will not only include information on the condition of a certain aspect of education but will also offer analytical commentary to help readers understand underlying forces.

Integrative reports are designed to cut across all four conceptual areas. These occasional reports will link data from the four conceptual areas to a developmental model of school improvement. The model suggests a set of realistic expectations regarding what kinds of school changes to anticipate at what points in time. The consortium has just released its first integrative report.

The research agenda also addressed reporting formats. Written reports make liberal use of graphics and creative formats. The first two survey reports were distributed as an insert in the local publication *Catalyst,* which is distributed to thirteen thousand people, including all principals, local school council members, reform groups, and professionals. Other vehicles used to communicate the consortium's research findings include small group briefings, informal conversations, workshops and conferences, and press releases and press conferences. For the teacher survey, schools received a report of their individual results. To help prepare school staff and local school councils to analyze their results, the NCREL worked with the consortium to develop a guidebook to and a video presentation of the teacher survey results (see Easton and Bennett, this volume, for details).

Organizing to Advance the Research Agenda

The consortium is a small organization with a few core professional staff. Currently, we have two and one-half full-time senior professional staff and the equivalent of approximately two full-time research associates working on various projects. The core staff provides most of the technical expertise in survey research, data management, and statistical analysis.

In addition, the consortium has developed a data archive on schooling in Chicago. The data archive is a large, complex relational data base containing information on school characteristics; student characteristics, program participation, test scores, and other information; survey data from consortium studies; data from other sources in the city; and U.S. Census Bureau data. The data archive is an integral part of the statistical analyses and reports that the consortium generates. To promote the involvement of multiple investigators in the research on Chicago schools, procedures are being developed to share these data. Researchers can obtain data sets tailored for their analyses. Data storage and use are subject to consortium policies and procedures for safeguarding the confidentiality of individuals and schools.

The consortium's major activities are undertaken as cooperative efforts among local institutions and individuals. For example, two of the codirectors (John Q. Easton and Albert L. Bennett) work part-time for the consortium, maintaining their primary appointments elsewhere. The consortium is structured to encourage the voluntaristic and collaborative spirit that has marked its activities to date.

To implement the research agenda, the consortium is in the process of establishing a study panel for each of the major topic areas. Each panel will stimulate research in its area, synthesize ongoing work, continue to refine issues through the stakeholder process, and promote continuing discussion around the city. Through these panels, the consortium will directly address activities suggested by the research agenda. These include development of an indicator system to assess progress in each of the four major areas and regular reporting on the condition of education in Chicago and related support activities, such as data archiving and public use surveys. In other cases, the consortium's primary function is to help individuals and groups undertake relevant studies and to promote broad dissemination and discussion of the results.

University faculty play a key role by participating in the implementation of the research agenda and serving on the consortium panels. Similarly, researchers in advocacy groups and community organizations help to shape the research agenda and have a strong interest in promoting consideration of the study results.

There is a special role for researchers whose professional affiliations are with state and local government. It is hard to envision the consortium work proceeding very far without the cooperation and genuine interest of state and local officials. In return, consortium studies can directly assist them in their role of advising key policymakers. More generally, full scrutiny and fair reporting are fundamental to maintaining community trust in our public institutions, and the consortium provides a vehicle for officials to execute this responsibility.

Finally, the foundation community plays a strategic role. In order to ensure full, balanced, and independent scrutiny of the reform process, it is vital to enlist multiple sources of support around these research activities.

Major Activities

In addition to developing the research agenda, which identified the central issues in advancing school reform and established a long-term plan of inquiry, the consortium has undertaken two major studies. The first was a survey of elementary school teachers in Chicago (Easton and others, 1991). Under the umbrella of the consortium, the following organizations collaborated to carry out the survey: Chicago Panel on Public School Policy and Finance; Center for School Improvement, University of Chicago; College of Education, University of Illinois at Chicago; Chicago Teachers Union; and Department of Research, Evaluation, and Planning of the

Chicago public schools. The survey asked teachers about school reform and its governance, the quality of their school communities, and teaching, instructional change, and professional development. Eighty-five percent ($N = 401$) of the city's elementary schools participated, with an average response rate of 78 percent. A citywide report was distributed through *Catalyst*, and, as mentioned above, individual school reports were returned to schools.

In 1992, the consortium launched its second major study, a survey of all elementary and high school principals in Chicago (Bennett and others, 1992). Eight organizations formed the task force for this survey: Chicago Principals Association; Center for School Improvement, University of Chicago; Chicago Panel on Public School Policy and Finance; Northeastern Illinois University; University of Illinois at Chicago; National-Louis University; and Department of Research, Evaluation, and Planning of the Chicago public schools. The survey asked questions about principals' reactions to reform and the new governance structure; human resources in the school, relations with parents, community, and the central and district offices; efforts to restructure schools; and the principal's role. Eighty-three percent ($N = 457$) of the principals responded; the report was distributed through *Catalyst* and received considerable attention in the local media and some print coverage elsewhere (see Easton and Bennett, this volume, for a detailed discussion of both projects).

Reflections on the First Two and One-Half Years

Perhaps the most fundamental lesson from the past two and one-half years is that a federation of diverse organizations can effectively collaborate to carry out policy research and engage stakeholder groups in the process. Although scholars have written about pluralistic policy research and stakeholder-based evaluation, and particular agencies have involved stakeholders in the design of evaluations (Henry, Dickey, and Areson, 1991; Baizerman and Compton, 1992; Stockdill, Duhon-Sells, Olson, and Patton, 1992; Madison, 1992), the consortium represents a unique implementation of these principles. It is essentially an assembly of researchers, some from the school system, others from universities, and still others who have ties to various stakeholder groups. This structure permits the consortium to directly engage researchers and stakeholders from the point of design to the final interpretation of results—a direct application of the principles outlined by Dewey (1927) and more recently elaborated by Weiss (1983), Stake (1980), Guba and Lincoln (1989), and Coleman, Bartot, Lewin-Epstein, and Olson (1979).

Our experience so far indicates that collaborative research produces both theoretical and practical benefits. In terms of the theoretical benefits, establishment of a work group to conduct a study brings multiple points of view to the effort from the very outset. In addition, there is a continuing effort to reach out to additional stakeholders and engage them in our work. For both the teacher and principal surveys, stakeholder groups suggested concepts and issues to explore and reviewed draft questionnaires. The resulting questionnaires were far more inclusive and interesting than they would have been without the participation of the various groups. During the data analysis phase, meetings were held with stakeholders to discuss presentation and interpretation of results. As a result, in some instances additional analyses were undertaken to clarify ambiguous points, new presentation formats were developed, and multiple interpretations were given for the same results.

With respect to reporting and dissemination, the consortium structure provides a bridge to policymakers, other researchers, administrators, teachers, and parents and other community members. Member organizations can share information with their own groups and collaborate with others on special projects. For example, NCREL, the University of Chicago, and the University of Illinois at Chicago cooperated on the videotape and guidebook to promote use of school-level results of the teacher survey. Because of their continuing involvement, member organizations can act as soon as results are available. Face-to-face briefings of practitioners and policymakers can be arranged through members' existing networks.

A significant advantage of pluralistic policy research is that it can reduce the costs of data collection. Although the stakeholder process adds time and complexity to the research activity and places new skill demands on the staff, it also helps to facilitate data collection. Stakeholders not only want information but also are often willing to work to get it. The school system's Department of Research, Planning, and Evaluation played an invaluable role in data collection for the teacher survey, and the Chicago Teachers Union worked very hard to encourage a high response rate. Given that thirteen thousand teachers completed the survey, the joint efforts of these two organizations saved considerable expenses in field costs, receipt control, and data processing.

Furthermore, the involvement of stakeholders in the design and conduct of the surveys boosts the response rate. We have already mentioned the key role of the Chicago Teachers Union in the teachers' survey. The consortium staff simply could not follow up with thousands of teachers. Rather, it was the encouragement by union leaders, regular mention of the survey at delegates' meetings, and reminders through routine communication channels that led to the extensive participation of the teachers.

Similarly, to get a high completion rate for the principal survey, we relied on principals who served on our advisory committee as well as on existing consortium networks. Reminder calls were made by other principals, university faculty, advocacy groups, graduate students, and basically anyone who knew a principal who had not yet submitted his or her questionnaire.

On balance, there are also difficulties with this approach. The consortium is competing with many other projects for the time of both researchers and stakeholders. Consequently, considerable effort is needed to plan efficient meetings and facilitate broad-based involvement. In addition, the task of conducting a study with committee oversight requires vigorous management and scheduling. Generally, the consortium staff takes responsibility for this task. The point is that pluralistic policy research requires a staff with a healthy mix of research, policy analysis, management, communication, and interpersonal skills.

Conclusion

Thousands of people in Chicago are involved in a massive effort to improve schooling. The reform is aimed at strengthening the participation of parents and citizens in their schools. At the same time, power and authority over the schools is widely dispersed. These circumstances call for a research approach that is broadly inclusive and reflects the democratic spirit of the reform effort.

The consortium, in its work on assessing school reform and school improvement in Chicago, seeks to achieve a productive blend of rigorous social science and vital democratic activity. The ultimate goal is to strengthen and sustain a more informed public discourse about education in the city—an ongoing discourse from the policy centers of the state, to the city center in the Loop, to the central administrative headquarters, to the 550 individual school communities, each of which is striving to become a vibrant, self-guided, neighborhood institution.

References

Baizerman, M., and Compton, D. "From Respondent and Informant to Consultant and Participant: The Evolution of a State Agency Policy Evaluation." In A. M. Madison (ed.), *Minority Issues in Program Evaluation.* New Directions for Program Evaluation, no. 53. San Francisco: Jossey-Bass, 1992.

Barber, B. B. *Strong Democracy: Participatory Politics for a New Age.* Berkeley and Los Angeles: University of California Press, 1984.

Bennett, A. L., and others. *Charting Reform: The Principals' Perspective.* Chicago: Consortium on Chicago School Research, 1992.

Bryk, A. S. (ed.). *Stakeholder-Based Evaluation.* New Directions for Program Evaluation, no. 17. San Francisco: Jossey-Bass, 1983.

Bryk, A. S., and Sebring, P. A. *Achieving School Reform in Chicago: What We Need to Know.* Chicago: Consortium on Chicago School Research, 1991.

Coleman, J. S., Bartot, V., Lewin-Epstein, N., and Olson, L. *Policy Issues and Research Design.* Washington, D.C.: National Center for Education Statistics, 1979.

Dewey, J. *The Public and Its Problems.* Troy, Mo.: Holt, Rinehart & Winston, 1927.

Easton, J. Q., and others. *Charting Reform: The Teachers' Turn.* Chicago: Consortium on Chicago School Research, 1991.

Guba, E. G., and Lincoln, Y. S. *Fourth-Generation Evaluation.* Newbury Park, Calif.: Sage, 1989.

Henry, G. T., Dickey, K. C., and Areson, J. C. "Stakeholder Participation in Educational Performance Monitoring Systems." *Educational Evaluation and Policy Analysis*, 1991, *13* (2), 177–188.

House, E. R. *Evaluating with Validity*. Newbury Park, Calif.: Sage, 1980.

Madison, A. M. "Primary Inclusion of Culturally Diverse Minority Program Participants in the Evaluation Process." In A. M. Madison (ed.), *Minority Issues in Program Evaluation*. New Directions for Program Evaluation, no. 53. San Francisco: Jossey-Bass, 1992.

Patton, M. Q. *Utilization Focused Evaluation*. Newbury Park, Calif.: Sage, 1978.

Shadish, W. R., Cook, T. D., and Leviton, L. C. *Foundations of Program Evaluation: Theories of Practice*. Newbury Park, Calif.: Sage, 1991.

Stake, R. E. "Program Evaluation, Particularly Responsive Evaluation." In W. B. Dockrell and D. Hamilton (eds.), *Rethinking Educational Research*. London: Hodder and Stoughton, 1980.

Stockdill, S. H., Duhon-Sells, R. M., Olson, R. A., and Patton, M. Q. "Voices in the Design and Evaluation of a Multicultural Education Program: A Developmental Approach." In A. M. Madison (ed.), *Minority Issues in Program Evaluation*. New Directions for Program Evaluation, no. 53. San Francisco: Jossey-Bass, 1992.

Weiss, C. H. *Evaluation Research: Methods for Assessing Program Effectiveness*. Englewood Cliffs, N.J.: Prentice Hall, 1972.

Weiss, C. H. "The Stakeholder Approach to Evaluation: Origins and Promise." In A. S. Bryk (ed.), *Stakeholder-Based Evaluation*. New Directions for Program Evaluation, no. 17. San Francisco: Jossey-Bass, 1983.

Weiss, C. H., and Bucuvalas, M. J. *Social Science Research and Decision Making*. New York: Columbia University Press, 1980.

PENNY A. SEBRING is senior research associate, Department of Education, University of Chicago and codirector of the Consortium on Chicago School Research.

ANTHONY S. BRYK is professor of education at the University of Chicago, codirector of the consortium, and chair of its steering committee.

This chapter describes the development and the results of two major surveys on Chicago school reform.

School Reform: Chicago Teachers and Principals Respond

John Q. Easton, Albert L. Bennett

In 1991, the Consortium on Chicago School Research conducted a survey of Chicago public school (CPS) elementary teachers (Easton and others, 1991), and, in 1992, the consortium surveyed both elementary and secondary school principals (Bennett and others, 1992). Because of the widespread interest in Chicago about school reform (see Hess, 1991; O'Connell, 1991), both surveys generated significant interest, from researchers and others willing to work on them, from teachers and principals eager to express their views, and from the public and the schools wishing to hear what their teachers and principals had to say.

Designing and Conducting the Surveys

The procedures for conducting these surveys emerged as we developed the teacher survey. Several members of an ad hoc data archiving committee of the consortium agreed to undertake the first survey and thereby established a pattern of creating "work groups" to conduct specific projects. Under the umbrella of the consortium, the work groups, or different subgroups of them, created the surveys, distributed them, analyzed the results, wrote the reports, and distributed the findings. The teacher survey work group included a researcher from the Chicago Panel on Public School Policy and Finance (a nonprofit education research and advocacy organization), a researcher from the CPS System, an education specialist from the Chicago Teachers Union, a consortium staff member, and professors from the University of Chicago and the University of Illinois at Chicago. The principal survey work group included representatives of the same groups

NEW DIRECTIONS FOR PROGRAM EVALUATION, no. 59, Fall 1993 © Jossey-Bass Publishers

as well as the Chicago Principals Association (replacing the teachers union), National-Louis University, Northeastern Illinois University, and Roosevelt University. The principal survey work group was also assisted by a research advisory group of local researchers and an external consultant.

Both surveys had similar goals: to collect high-quality information on the attitudes and experiences of teachers and principals in relation to school reform, their work, their school community, and instruction; to create indicators of progress toward certain CPS systemwide goals; and to report the results widely. This information was intended to stimulate informal dialogue about the implementation of school reform and the progress of school improvement in Chicago.

The work groups, following the consortium's commitment to pluralism (Sebring and Bryk, this volume), were determined to use a stakeholder process (Bryk, 1983) to develop and administer their surveys. Toward that end, they consulted regularly with several different groups. For the teacher survey, the most influential of these stakeholders included members of the Chicago Teachers Union. Between twelve and fifteen teachers met several times to review material and provide guidance on the content of the survey (including review of specific items) and on the logistics of administering the survey and, finally, to assist in interpreting the survey results. Similarly, the principal survey work group consulted with a group of principals. Both work groups met with CPS central office administrators (including deputy and associate superintendents in the areas of teacher personnel, curriculum and instruction, school reform, and school services); the principal survey work group met with teachers, and the teacher survey work group met with principals.

Both survey work groups looked to extant surveys for items. About half of the questions on the teacher survey came from known national surveys; the work group wrote the other items. The principal survey work group wrote more than half of the items. (Technical documentation, available from the consortium, indicates the source of all items.) Stakeholder and advisory groups reviewed all newly written items.

Data Collection and Response Rates

Because of the large number of CPS elementary school teachers (over eighteen thousand), the teacher survey work group faced a substantial logistical problem with survey administration. We wanted to administer the survey to groups of teachers but did not know the best procedure for bringing teachers together. Several stakeholder groups recommended or endorsed the method that we eventually chose: For each school, a teacher and the principal were asked to jointly invite teachers to a meeting where they would fill out the survey. Although we recommended this procedure to schools, we do not know how many followed it. The CPS Department of Research, Evaluation, and Planning coordinated the distribution and receipt of the teacher survey and scanned the completed surveys.

With only 550 principals, the principal survey work group had an easier job, although again we preferred to administer the survey to groups of principals. In most cases, principals completed the survey during district service center meetings. In other cases, surveys were mailed directly to principals' homes and returned to the consortium in self-addressed stamped envelopes.

The consortium conducted relatively extensive publicity campaigns for both surveys. The Chicago Teachers Union urged teachers to participate in its newsletters and at delegates' meetings. The work group wrote to all subdistrict superintendents, principals, chairs of the local school councils (LSCs), and chairs of the Professional Personnel Advisory Committees (PPACs; groups of teachers who advise the LSCs on curriculum and instructional matters) to request participation. The school system also endorsed the survey and asked principals to assist with survey administration. All teachers received a brief letter signed by the general superintendent of schools, the president of the Chicago Board of Education, and the president of the Chicago Teachers Union.

The principal survey work group followed similar strategies in 1992. We wrote to all principals ahead of time and then asked a network of principals to send letters to colleagues urging participation.

Evidently our strategies harnessed teacher and principal willingness to describe their experiences with school reform and their work; both surveys received very high numbers of responses. The overall response rate on the teacher survey was 70 percent. Our reporting is based on the 401 elementary schools (out of 473) that obtained a response rate of 50 percent or greater. In these schools, the combined rate was 78 percent. Teachers in these schools received an individual school profile, which is described below. For the principal survey, the response rate was even higher: 83 percent, or 457 out of 550, completed the survey. They will receive an individual, confidential profile of their responses.

Results of the Teacher Survey

The teacher survey results are organized into three categories: views on school reform, views on school communities, and views on instructional change.

Views on School Reform. The majority of teachers responded positively to questions about school reform and indicated at least some optimism that their respective schools were improving. On balance, teachers were positive about reform, but a minority was not supportive. For example, 20 percent of teachers strongly agreed with the statement "Since reform, I feel better about working in this school." Another 36 percent agreed, yet 26 percent disagreed and 18 percent strongly disagreed. Clearly, there were pockets of negative attitudes toward reform. In general, however, teachers did not report increased problems in their schools, including more conflict, more disruptions, and worsening relations between school and community. At the same time, teachers were evenly split as to whether positive consequences, such as more cooperation and greater parental involvement, had occurred since school reform.

Overall, teachers in about three-quarters of the schools could be characterized as positive about reform. That is, they had positive attitudes toward reform, did not observe negative consequences, and saw positive trends emerging. In 62 schools (out of 401 with a 50 percent or greater response rate), teachers were solidly "proreform." These schools are located throughout the different neighborhoods and community areas of the city. Teachers in another 241 schools were more positive than negative. In 89 schools, teachers were somewhat negative, and teachers in the remaining 9 schools reported clearly negative attitudes.

The survey asked many questions about school governance and topics specific to Chicago school reform, including the LSCs, PPACs, and school improvement plans (SIPs). Teachers responded positively to these questions: Two-thirds believed that the teacher members of their LSCs represented them fairly, 60 percent said that PPACs increased teacher involvement in policy-making, and over 68 percent were helping to implement their SIPs.

Teachers' answers to items about SIPs raised questions about interpretation and appropriate standards for judging responses. In our citywide report, we did not offer single interpretations of many findings but rather presented different perspectives. In the case of the questions about SIPs, between two-thirds and three-quarters of teachers answered positively about their knowledge of the plans, their involvement in developing and implementing the plans, and their optimism in the plans' success. On the one hand, it could be argued that *all* teachers should be familiar with their SIPs and that *all* should be helping to implement them. From this point of view, any response rate below 90 percent could be considered low. On the other hand, it could be argued that collaborative planning is a radical departure from past practices in CPSs and that for any sizable portion of teachers to be involved represents a major change. From this of view, any response rate over a token level (say 20 percent) could be considered positive. In the interest of informing further discussion and without taking a specific position, we reported these differing points of view raised by stakeholders.

We examined teachers' responses about school reform and the school governance components (LSC, PPAC, and SIP) in relation to several characteristics about the schools where they teach, including racial compositions, student mobility rates, student achievement levels prior to the implementation of school reform, total enrollment of each school, and concentrations of low-income students. The results showed that the size of the school (total student enrollment) was most strongly related to how teachers felt about reform and whether the LSC, PPAC, and SIP were working well. Teachers in small schools (350 students or fewer, which is small for Chicago but average statewide) had more positive responses than teachers in larger schools. Although we know of no other research linking the effects of school size to reform implementation, other research has related smaller school size to positive effects (for example, Bryk, Lee, and Smith, 1990; Fowler and Walberg, 1991).

Student achievement levels were also somewhat related to teacher responses, with higher responses in schools with higher prereform achievement. Other school-level characteristics were not related to how teachers responded to these reform and governance questions. Individual teacher characteristics (race, gender, and education background) were also unrelated to teacher responses about reform and school governance.

Views on School Communities. The survey contained two pages of questions related to the quality of their schools and work conditions. These topics included safety, order, sense of mission, teacher collegiality, parental and community involvement, and teacher influence. We grouped these into ten clusters. Each cluster consisted of between two and seven items (typically three to five), both conceptually and statistically related, and had acceptable internal consistency as measured by Cronbach's alpha.

Some of the more important findings are the following: One-third of the teachers believed that their students do not feel safe around the school, and nearly one-quarter said that they do not feel safe coming from and going to school. Since a sense of safety is a minimal prerequisite to teaching and learning, the fact that a substantial portion of teachers and students do not feel safe is a cause for concern.

More than one-half of the teachers said that student misbehavior interferes with their teaching. Of the ten school quality clusters, this one received the lowest ratings from teachers. Clearly, many teachers see the safety issue as a significant school problem.

Sixty-six percent of the teachers agreed that staff members support and encourage one another. Nearly 60 percent agreed that they have influence on the decisions that affect them. However, teachers indicated less control over specific school policies: 52 percent have a great deal or some influence determining the content of staff development, but only 44 percent have a great deal or some influence in establishing the school curriculum. Only 23 percent influence the planning of overall school budgets.

Responses to the school leadership questions were among the most positive of the ten school quality clusters. Almost 75 percent of the teachers believed that the administration and teaching staff collaborate in running the school; over 70 percent indicated that staff are encouraged and supported in their schools.

In the minds of many CPS elementary teachers, they are not receiving the support that they need from parents to do their jobs. Almost 80 percent of the teachers reported that their schools make an effort to reach out to the communities, but fewer than 50 percent reported that people in the communities try to help the schools. Although almost 60 percent of teachers said that parents respect them, only 50 percent felt that they receive a great deal of support from parents for the work they do.

Like governance, school quality is also related to school size. Teachers in small schools gave significantly higher ratings in these areas than did teachers in larger schools. The achievement level of the school prior to school reform is also significantly related to quality clusters, with higher ratings from the higher-performance schools. As achievement levels drop, so also do the quality reports, showing that the schools most in need of academic improvements are working from the weakest organizational bases.

Views on Instructional Change. *Charting Reform: The Teachers' Turn* (Easton and others, 1991) contained questions on teachers' feelings about their work, about instructional change, and about professional growth. Teachers expressed high expectations for students' learning: about two-thirds believed that their students are capable of learning the required materials, yet two-thirds also believed that students have habits and attitudes that interfere with their learning. Teachers seemed to believe that students have the innate ability to succeed but that the home and community interfere.

Teachers also expressed a very strong sense of their own competence: almost 95 percent felt competent teaching reading and mathematics. Likewise, most believed that they are making a difference in their students' lives. These positive feelings of competence and efficacy contrast sharply with student achievement in Chicago, where only 10 percent of the schools have achievement test scores at or above national norms.

Although the teachers were moderately optimistic that their schools will improve, fewer than half said that their instructional procedures have changed or will change. Teachers apparently believed that improvements will occur elsewhere, not in their classrooms. Teachers who had a higher sense of efficacy and who were more involved in school governance were more likely to report changes in their classroom practices. These teachers were more often found in schools where other teachers expressed positive attitudes about reform and where they reported having a great deal of influence over school decision making. In addition, it is encouraging to note that more instructional change is reported in schools with lower achievement levels and higher incidence of behavioral problems.

In sum, teachers displayed moderately positive attitudes toward Chicago school reform, yet they indicated little inclination toward changing their own instructional practices. This finding underscores the notion that the reform has altered school governance practices significantly in Chicago but has had little effect on other educational practices. The survey provided strong evidence that teachers in small schools are more highly engaged in school reform than are teachers in larger schools.

We believe that the teacher survey results have significantly influenced citywide discussions about CPSs. Newspaper editorials and published opinions have pointed to the survey findings on the positive correlates of small schools. Small schools that successfully fought threats of closure (for "efficiency's sake") cited the survey results in their testimony to the Chicago Board of Education. In addition, many large schools in Chicago are creating "schools-within-schools" to try to reap the benefits that come with smaller schools.

The survey results also engendered discussion about the need for instructional changes. We found that school governance reform was succeeding in the majority of schools, but there was much less evidence of change in how teachers and students interact. Since the survey, we have heard more calls for action for improvements in and restructuring of teachers' work and classroom teaching.

Individual School Reports

Several months after the citywide teacher survey report was released, all of the teachers in the 401 elementary schools that achieved a 50 percent or better response rate received an individual school profile. Each profile was divided into three major sections: school governance, school quality, and instructional practices. For each cluster (and for all supporting items), the report provided the citywide average score, the school average score, and the average score of a group of similar schools. These comparison schools (listed by name on the school report) were of roughly equal size and had comparable numbers of low-income students and prereform achievement levels.

In order to encourage serious discussions of these individual school reports, the consortium and the North Central Regional Educational Laboratory created support materials, including a videotape that highlighted the citywide survey results and portrayed a group of teachers discussing a school's teacher survey profile. The Chicago Teachers Union, the University of Illinois at Chicago, the Center for School Improvement at the University of Chicago, and several other organizations organized training sessions for facilitators who would work with schools to discuss and analyze their results. The survey findings provided a vehicle for schools to reflect on their own states of reform and what they need to address next.

Principal Survey Results

The principal survey results are described in four sections: school reform and governance, human resources in Chicago schools, school restructuring, and principals' roles and school leadership.

School Reform and Governance. Like the teachers, a majority of principals expressed a positive view of school reform and its new governance structures. Moreover, the experience of the last three years seems to have dispelled their initial misgivings about the role and activities of the LSCs. The study also showed that principals' race or gender did not affect their perceptions, nor did the racial compositions, income distributions, or achievement levels of the schools they served.

More than 75 percent of the principals believed that their schools had improved since reform, and almost 66 percent expressed optimism that their schools will improve or continue to improve as a result of reform. Eighty percent of the respondents said they share with their LSCs a similar understanding of the principal's responsibilities and rights, and 61 percent believed that their LSCs have clear conceptions of the LSC's role and responsibilities. Most principals (76 percent) believed that the LSCs do not interfere with their authority and grant them sufficient autonomy and respect to get the job done. Almost 60 percent of principals felt that on all important matters they still make the final decisions.

A majority of principals (58 percent) agreed that the LSC contributes to academic improvements, and 55 percent considered the LSC an effective policy-making body. Although most principals felt that their LSCs had been fair and objective in conducting their performance evaluations, only 38 percent indicated that the LSCs had provided constructive suggestions for carrying out their job.

More than 80 percent of the respondents reported regular communication and cooperative relationships with their schools' PPACs. Almost 60 percent agreed that the PPAC helps to improve curriculum and instruction and contributes good ideas for school improvement. However, fewer than 50 percent of the principals said that the PPAC regularly makes reports to the LSC, suggesting that in many schools the PPAC-LSC relationship is weak.

More than three-quarters of respondents indicated that their LSCs had participated in developing the SIPs required by the Chicago School Reform Act of 1988. They also strongly agreed (80 percent) that the SIPs helped their schools focus on common goals, and two-thirds stated that the SIPs had already led to academic improvement.

Overall, 25 percent of principals awarded two or more areas of school governance (LSC, PPAC, or SIP) very high marks. Another 44 percent were very positive in one area and moderately positive in the other two. Twenty-one percent gave mixed ratings. Only 10 percent of principals offered consistently negative responses about their LSCs, PPACs, and SIPs. Schools with high ratings from principals tended to have higher levels of teacher collegiality and positive school-community relationships, as reported on the teacher survey. These schools also tended to have smaller student bodies, again suggesting that smaller schools foster effective governance and trust between parents and professionals. An analysis of elementary school results indicated that ratings on governance were not affected by geographical locations of the schools or by characteristics of the student bodies.

Human Resources in Chicago Schools. Principals expressed mixed feelings about their teaching staffs. While the majority saw their teachers as committed professionals, there were many exceptions. One-third of principals responded that a significant portion of teachers do not adequately teach reading and language arts. A little over half of the principals felt that most or almost all of their teachers have a good grasp of mathematics. Principals expressed even more concern about their teachers' ability to adequately teach social studies and science. These findings stand in striking contrast to the views of teachers as reported in the teacher survey: 95 percent of elementary school teachers indicated that they felt confident teaching reading, writing, and mathematics. The school reform act provided only partial remedies for these problems. While it brought new authority for principals to hire faculty of their choice, surveyed principals claimed that resources for staff development are inadequate and that the new procedures for removing incompetent teachers are still quite cumbersome.

Three-quarters of the principals agreed that there is a great deal of cooperation and mutual support among staff members and that almost two-thirds of teachers make efforts to coordinate their curricula with those of other grades. Sixty-six percent of the principals believed that almost all or most of their teachers feel responsible for student learning, and about 50 percent reported that half or fewer of their teachers take responsibility for school improvement.

Two-thirds of principals agreed with the statement "I have more autonomy in selecting teachers," and one-third reported taking advantage of this new power to hire new teachers, amounting to 20 percent or more of their faculties. However, virtually none of the principals felt that the new remediation procedures introduced by reform are helpful in removing nonperforming teachers.

When questioned about the percentage of teachers they would like to see leave, 60 percent of principals indicated 10 percent or fewer, or three or four teachers per school. Principals were divided on the question of whether the quality of the teaching force has improved since the beginning of reform: 37 percent agreed that it has, and 26 percent reported no improvement.

School Restructuring. One of the most positive findings of the survey is that reform has catalyzed much restructuring activity in a large number of schools, including some of the city's least-advantaged schools. The effects of school restructuring are most apparent through the addition of computer-learning facilities and the implementation of innovative teaching techniques in a significant number of schools. But the more in-depth restructuring—increased student involvement in planning and restructuring of teachers' work and role—has yet to occur in most schools. While more and stronger community ties have been established, one-third of the schools do not have regular contact with external education organizations. Such ties are most evident in schools where restructuring began before reform.

Principals reported that computers are now found in approximately 75 percent of schools. Other positive changes brought by restructuring are also becoming prevalent. For example, almost half of the principals reported implementation of innovative teaching techniques such as deep engagement of students in subject matter, making students active participants in the learning process, and assessment emphasizing student production of knowledge. However, the restructuring of teachers' work or role within the school has occurred in less than half of the schools, according to the principals.

Reform has been most successful in fostering the establishment of stronger ties between the communities and the schools. Sixty percent of principals reported moderate to extensive activity in this area, twice as much as what occurred prior to reform. Active, formal parent and community volunteer programs were reported by 79 percent of principals.

Reform appears to be stimulating change in some of the least-advantaged schools—those with predominantly low-income, minority students and low preform achievement levels. Other similarly disadvantaged schools reported minimal or no restructuring. Although one year earlier teachers reported less instructional change, the patterns of teachers' and principals' responses are similar. More instructional changes seems to be occurring in schools with the lowest achievement levels and the most problems with student misbehavior.

Principals' Roles and School Leadership. School reform brought substantial changes in school leadership. Of current Chicago school principals, 43 percent have been hired since reform, and almost all of these are new to the principalship (94 percent). Over 65 percent of these new principals agreed that school reform gave them the opportunity to become a principal.

Over 50 percent of the principals hired since reform are African American, and almost 60 percent are women. Since reform, the average age of principals has fallen: Prereform, the average age was fifty-two; it is now forty-six. New principals are most likely to be found in racially isolated schools and are more likely to be racially or ethnically matched with their schools.

Principals reported that they divided their time between four main activities: school management issues, instructional leadership efforts, work with local constituencies, and student activities. On average, principals said that they spend more than ten hours per week on each of these activities and work a total of almost sixty hours per week. However, they felt that their most critical concern—leadership for instructional improvement—is being displaced by managerial and administrative tasks.

Three-quarters of principals reported feeling overwhelmed by administrative demands. A sense of frustration also was evident among principals hired prior to reform, who indicated that their accountability for improving their schools has increased since reform, while they doubt that they have the necessary resources to effect improvements. Seventy-eight percent perceived that they are held more accountable for improving their schools since reform, but only 41 percent felt better about working in their schools since reform.

When asked about the most frustrating parts of their work, the principals mentioned paperwork demands (34 percent), not enough time and too much to do (21 percent), community politics (12 percent), and problems with entrenched, incompetent, or uncaring teachers (7 percent). In answer to the question "What would be your priorities for changing or adding to the current contract with the Chicago Teachers Union?" 42 percent of principals responded, "Make it easier to remove incompetent teachers."

Ninety-four percent of principals believed they are making a difference in the academic development of their students, 78 percent believed they have high status in their communities, and 77 percent felt satisfied most of the time. However, of principals hired prior to reform, 64 percent felt that they have less prestige, and 79 percent indicated that they have less respect from the public than they did prior to reform.

Principals' frustrations are illustrated by the data on how long they expected to remain in the job. Over 40 percent of principals were planning to leave the principalship in five years, and 75 percent planned to be gone in ten years or less. Even among the principals hired since reform, 57 percent planned to leave in ten years or less.

In summary, principals offered a generally positive account of the state of school reform. Local governance appears to be working well in the majority of schools. Principals also reported that, in general, PPACs are functioning and that principals have been able to select a substantial number of teachers of their own choosing. Reform has also triggered a burst of restructuring activities in a large number of schools, especially in schools where LSCs have hired new, energetic principals.

Reports about the human resources in the schools are less positive than the governance and restructuring reports. Both principals and teachers need sustained staff development, but current resources are inadequate for these needs. Principals also felt that the current processes for removing incompetent teachers are overly constrained.

By all accounts, most principals exhibit enormous energy and dedication. Despite working long hours, they are still unable to devote enough time to instructional leadership. Principals are held personally accountable for improvement in student achievement, but they lack critical resources and authority to advance such improvement. The time demands associated with school management and work with local constituencies have increased substantially, but little change has occurred in cumbersome bureaucratic procedures. Significant school improvement seems highly unlikely without active leadership from principals. Thus, their generally positive accounts of school reform are tempered by their reports about the conflicts and constraints in their new role. These constraints point out the need for making the current demands on principals more manageable.

Conclusion

Each of the surveys described here accomplished its goals of informing public discussion, providing indicators of reform implementation, and assisting school-level planning. Because of their high technical quality, high response rates, and multipartisan perspective, the surveys provided Chicago with the most comprehensive information available about the status of school reform, as well as other information about the schools and their teachers and principals. Some of the surveys' key findings, such as, the importance of school size (small is better), have become part of the local vocabulary for school improvement. Other findings, such as, principals' concerns about providing staff development for teachers (always problematic in Chicago), are being examined with a new perspective and are likely to affect policy in these areas. The consortium has brought together a diversity of stakeholders to work on issues of great importance to CPSs. So far, they have completed two significant survey projects that would have been very difficult for any of the consortium's individual members to have conducted alone.

References

Bennett, A. L., and others. *Charting Reform: The Principals' Perspective*. Chicago: Consortium on Chicago School Research, 1992.

Bryk, A. S. (ed.). *Stakeholder-Based Evaluation*. New Directions for Program Evaluation, no. 17. San Francisco: Jossey-Bass, 1983.

Bryk, A. S., Lee, V., and Smith, J. "High School Organization and Its Effect on Teachers and Students: An Interpretive Summary of the Research." In W. H. Clune and J. F. Witte (eds.), *Choice and Control in American Education*. Philadelphia: Falmer Press, 1990.

Easton, J. Q., and others. *Charting Reform: The Teachers' Turn*. Chicago: Consortium on Chicago School Research, 1991.

Fowler, W. J., and Walberg, H. J. "School Size, Characteristics, and Outcomes." *Educational Evaluation and Policy Analysis*, 1991, *13*, 189–202.

Hess, G. A., Jr. *School Restructuring, Chicago Style*. Newbury Park, Calif.: Corwin Press, 1991.

O'Connell, M. *School Reform Chicago Style: How Citizens Organized to Change Public Policy*. Chicago: Center for Neighborhood Technology, 1991.

JOHN Q. EASTON is director of monitoring and research at the Chicago Panel on Public School Policy and Finance and codirector of the Consortium on Chicago School Research.

ALBERT L. BENNETT is dean of the Evelyn T. Stone University College and professor of education at Roosevelt University, Chicago. He is also codirector of the consortium.

The effort to restructure the Chicago public schools is examined as it is played out in fourteen representative schools. While systemwide structural change is impressive and resources have been redirected to the school level, the authors argue that schools must now focus on pragmatic planning for instructional change.

Case Studies of Chicago Schools Under Reform

G. Alfred Hess, Jr., Susan Leigh Flinspach, Susan P. Ryan

Evaluation of a massive reform effort that spans more than 540 local units, 45,000 employees, and 410,000 students requires a comprehensive re-search design that includes extensive quantitative tracking of systemwide data and a sampling of individual units for more intensive qualitative investigation. Based on a decade of both quantitative (Hess and Lauber, 1985, who tracked 100,000 students through high school to determine longitudinal dropout rates) and qualitative (Hess and others, 1987, an ethnographic, matched-pairs, effective schools type of study of eight Chicago high schools) research into the Chicago public schools, the Chicago Panel on Public School Policy and Finance created a five-year research design to track the implementation of school reform legislation in the city. The design included a large-scale quantitative analysis of school improvement and an intensive qualitative analysis of the implementation of reform. The panel, working with Anthony S. Bryk at the University of Chicago Center for School Improvement and with the Department of Research, Evaluation, and Planning of the Chicago public schools, ana-lyzed the achievement test scores of elementary school students. The purpose of this study was to measure change at the school level, identify improving schools, and develop a better knowledge of the correlates of school improvement (Easton, Dean, and Bryk, 1992; Dean, Bryk, and

The authors are indebted to their colleagues on the Chicago Panel on Public School Policy and Finance, whose efforts are summarized in this chapter.

Easton, 1992). This study utilized hierarchical linear modeling (Bryk and Raudenbush, 1992).

The Chicago panel also is an active participant in the Consortium on Chicago School Research, which combines the efforts of the public school system, the major universities in the Chicago area, and a number of research-oriented nonprofit agencies. John Q. Easton, the panel's director of monitoring and research, serves on the steering committee of the consortium and acted as chair of the work group that surveyed 18,000 elementary school teachers at the end of the second year of reform (Easton and others, 1991a; see Easton and Bennett, this volume). He also has been a key contributor to the consortium's 1992 survey of more than 450 Chicago principals at the end of the third year of reform. These surveys provide additional quantitative data for assessing reform across the whole system and for informing the panel's achievement-based study.

Complementing these large-scale quantitative studies is a more intensive qualitative study of fourteen representative schools, randomly selected from a stratified sample, including four high schools and ten elementary schools. Staff from the Chicago panel have been studying these schools for three years, attending every local school council (LSC) meeting, observing teachers' meetings, and interviewing principals, LSC chairs, and chairs of the Professional Personnel Advisory Committees (PPACs; the teachers' vehicles for input into the reform process at their schools). At the end of each year, panel staff produced summaries of LSC operations for the previous year.

The opportunity to study a major policy initiative to reform an urban school system is a mixed blessing. Aside from the tremendous effort that it requires, the task of assessing a public policy initiative of this scale presents daunting challenges, especially when approached from an anthropological perspective. Ethnographic studies are typically small-scale, involve a single site, often are restricted to a small number of informants, and frequently involve a culture that is exotic to the researcher. Anthropologists tend to be happier studying simpler societies in their own contexts or marginalized groups on the edges of the mainstream culture. This propensity frequently leads them to study the dissonance experienced by minority subgroups, whether based on race, gender, or ethnicity. And this propensity has produced some of the very best work in anthropology, such as John Ogbu's (1978) *Minority Education and Caste: The American System in Cross-Cultural Perspective.*

But assessment of the effects of the school reform movement in Chicago is complex and huge in scope and requires a focus on the mainstream cultural core, within which our cities now operate. Since the last decade, there has been a growing interest in anthropology to examine the American mainstream (for example, Harris, 1981; Holland and Eisenhart, 1990). It seems that most anthropologists who study the American mainstream do so from a postpositivist orientation, perhaps to achieve the same distance and otherness that anthropologists bring to their studies of the exotic and the marginalized. As anthropologists involved in policy-relevant research on the Chicago public schools, the task of assessing the effects of the Chicago reform effort required critical reflection on our own perspective.

At one point in our qualitative study of the fourteen representative schools, our research team was going over a draft report that we were preparing together to describe the status of school improvement plans (SIPs) in those schools. Our task had been to analyze the schools' planning documents to see what patterns might be emerging and to assess them for their likely effects on the schools. We were discussing why we were preparing this report at that point, just two years into a five-year study of reform implementation. We talked about our hopes that these fourteen schools, and others across the city to whom we would distribute our study report, would read the report, would see what they had planned and what they had omitted that others had included, and would then *change* their plans and their future behavior. The report was not intended to simply catalogue what had been happening in the school improvement dimension of Chicago school reform. The report was intended to critique the plans and to instigate change in the very process that we were studying!

Now, for those familiar with the works of Habermas (1971, 1978) and anthropologists such as Marcus and Fischer (1986), such a suggestion does not sound so terribly radical. But for positivistically trained graduate students and researchers, it was a shocking moment to realize what we had been lured into doing under the guise of a part-time research job in a nonprofit, policy-relevant agency. This crossover from theory to practice defines one major challenge facing anthropologists who work in the education arena today. Are we there merely to catalogue what is going on, to sit back in our armchairs and postulate theories, or are we also there to try to have a profound impact on how schooling is done in America? Do we simply catalogue? Or do we also critique? And if we critique, is that critique detached and dispassionate? Or is it engaged and active? (For detailed examination of the issues of policy-relevant qualitative research, see Hess, 1992a.)

The panel's study of fourteen representative schools is clearly designed to track the implementation of school reform and to provide an in-depth look into the struggles encountered by LSCs as they try to improve their schools. But the effort is also dedicated to presenting the studied schools, and all others in the district, with insights into the implementation process and with recommendations for improved implementation. Our research is not designed to be simply a five-year, nonintrusive study that results in a summative report. It is intended to provide assistance to schools across the city as they struggle to reform themselves and to provide insight to policymakers and the general public on the progress of reform in the country's third largest school system. The panel has produced more than a dozen reports on the progress of the reform effort (for example, Easton and Storey, 1990a, 1990b; Easton and others, 1991b, 1992) and a series of data books that provide quantifiable information on student characteristics and achievement for every school in the system. But since this reform effort has been called the most radical effort ever attempted to transform the governance of a major urban school system, firmly rooted in a democratic, rather than professionalized, approach to school improvement (Elmore, 1991), it is important to provide such assessments to the national research community as well. Toward that end, panel staff also have reported the findings in conference papers (Ford, 1992; Ryan, 1992; Dean, Bryk, and Easton, 1992; Easton, Dean, and Bryk, 1992), book chapters (Hess and Easton, 1992; Hess, 1992d), and journal articles (Hess, 1991, 1992b, 1992c).

School Restructuring, Chicago Style: A Midway Report

Halfway through the initial five-year implementation period envisioned in the Chicago School Reform Act of 1988 (P.A. 85-1418), the panel released a report summarizing our studies to date (Hess, 1992e). We reported the following findings:

LSCs have been established and, for the most part, function successfully. LSCs were elected at all regular schools in October 1989. Despite initial chaos concerning places to meet and early expenditure decisions, they successfully adopted SIPs and local school budgets, and they evaluated principals and selected their leadership for the next four years. At 38 percent of Chicago schools, a new principal was selected. LSC attendance varied from school to school but, on average, was at about 70 percent, with principals attending most frequently. LSC chairs and teacher representatives had attendance rates above 80 percent, while community representatives and parents other than the chair were nearer to 60 percent. Although LSCs spent nearly one-third of their agendas on organizational matters, they also devoted one-third of their topics to dimensions of the school program. Building, finance, and personnel (primarily principal selection) dominated the remainder of their discussions. Efforts to increase parental involvement were discussed infrequently.

SIPs have focused more on add-ons than on alterations of the regular instructional programs of schools. In the first year of school improvement planning, most schools focused on solving practical problems such as overcrowding, student discipline, gang control, and low attendance rates. About one-quarter of the observed schools planned quite significant changes in their instructional programs, while another quarter approved very rudimentary plans. An analysis of the revised plans adopted in the second year showed that curriculum changes were most prevalent, pedagogical improvements next most frequent, followed by organizational and other changes (Easton and others, 1991b). About one-quarter of the studied schools were attempting changes that would impact all regular classroom instruction, while another quarter were planning changes in some classrooms. More frequently, schools were favoring add-on programs such as additional classes (art, music, science, or computer laboratories) and additional instruction (after school, before school, or summer school). Most add-ons can be implemented easily if money and new staff are available. Initiatives that affect the regular classroom experiences of students require significant commitment and time from teachers. One elementary school in particular, described in greater detail later, is emblematic of efforts to change regular classroom instruction. It is implementing Socratic seminars in an attempt to improve the content and intellectual level of classroom discussion, a literature-based reading program, extensive use of hands-on learning in mathematics, an experimental approach to science, and an innovative schoolwide writing program.

Principals have adopted new roles and are providing new leadership. As mentioned above, at least 38 percent of Chicago schools are now led by principals who were not in that position when reform began. A similar percentage of schools in the Chicago panel's study sample are now served by new principals. The selection process went smoothly in some schools, but others had a more difficult time in keeping their incumbent evaluation process objective and separate from the launching of a search for a new candidate. In some schools, the principal selection process so dominated their agendas that they could not conduct other business such as revising their SIPs or adopting school budgets. Principals during the initial years of reform found the time demands excessive. They were playing new roles, not all of which seemed appropriate. One principal complained that she now had to be a public relations figure, a referee among factions in her school, and a glorified clerk making lots of reports (Ford, 1992). But some principals also saw the reform effort as a source of greater opportunities, particularly relative to staff selection and to the additional support they received from highly involved LSC members, parents, and teachers.

Teachers have become increasingly involved in and positive about reform. Based on two surveys and interviews with a series of key school-level teacher leaders, it appears that teachers are now quite involved in reform at most schools. A small survey taken before the first LSC elections showed that teachers did not expect to be extensively involved in reform (Easton, 1989). They thought that increased parental involvement was the primary strength of the reform effort and worried that such involvement might lead to greater classroom interference. In a much more comprehensive survey of thirteen thousand elementary school teachers administered at the end of the second year of reform (Easton and others, 1991a), a majority of teachers responded positively to questions about school reform. In 62 schools, teachers were very positive about reform, while in another 241 they were moderately positive. In 89 schools, teachers were somewhat negative, while in 9 schools they were very negative. Teachers felt that they were fairly represented on LSCs and had increased involvement in policy-making, and they said that they were involved in implementing their schools' SIPs. Interviews in the panel's fourteen sampled schools indicated that teachers had a major role in determining their SIPs, which were generally accepted as proposed by teachers to the LSCs. Although the comprehensive survey indicated that teachers were mildly optimistic that their schools would improve, fewer than one-half indicated that their own instructional practices had changed or would change in the future.

Resources have been increasingly focused on the schools, with the greatest increases in schools enrolling the highest proportions of disadvantaged students. Between the 1988–89 school year, when the reform law was being enacted, and 1991–92, the Chicago public schools increased revenues by $403 million, mostly from increased local property tax receipts (state aid increased by only $25 million). Most of this money was reallocated to schools (primarily through state Chapter I). While nearly 840 administrative unit positions were eliminated, the number of school staff members increased by 3,365. In one-half of those positions, schools hired classroom aides; schools also added just over 1,000 teachers and other professional staff. Funds have been much more equitably allocated to schools to meet the needs of disadvantaged young people. In the year before school reform began, elementary schools with 90 to 99 percent low-income students averaged $500 less per pupil in expenditures than did schools with fewer than 30 percent low-income students. In 1991–92, the schools with the heaviest concentrations of low-income students had nearly $1,000 more per pupil than did those with the fewest disadvantaged pupils.

National school improvement efforts have "marched on Chicago" to assist many schools. In 1988, there were few national school improvement efforts working in Chicago schools. In 1992, there were more than 170 schools listed under various national reform efforts working in Chicago (see Hess, 1992e, appendix). While some of these efforts have a distinctly Chicago flavor (Paideia Program, Illinois Writing Project, and the federally supported desegregation program Project CANAL), others are products of major school reformers such as Ted Sizer (Coalition of Essential Schools), Hank Levin (Accelerated Schools Network), and James Comer (Comer School Development Program). These national efforts are providing valuable resources to schools and school staffs as they work to improve Chicago's schools. These efforts were largely unavailable to the city's schools prior to school reform.

It is still too early to see any changes in student achievement. School reform efforts in Chicago, at the midway point in the initial focus period, had little opportunity to become manifested in improved student achievement. The first year of the reform effort was designed to establish a LSC at every school and to develop improvement plans with supporting school budgets. Only in the second year did schools begin to implement changes; but during that year, one-half of the schools were still involved in the process of evaluating their incumbent principals and making leadership decisions for the next four years. The achievement tests available at reform's midway point had been taken only eight months into that second year and could not be expected to show any significant changes—and they did not show any. Other measures, such as dropout rates, continue to reflect prior years of neglect, while students who have experienced major changes under reform are still several years from graduation. Attendance rates for elementary schools remain flat; at the high school level, they declined slightly, reflecting closer recording scrutiny.

Overall, school reform was successfully launched; some schools are beginning to change in significant ways, but many more need to follow their lead. Despite the chaos created by fiscal mismanagement, the major elements of the Chicago School Reform Act have been successfully established. LSCs are functioning in almost all Chicago schools. SIPs are being debated by nearly twelve thousand people each month of the school year. In some schools, important efforts are underway to change the way in which instruction is carried on in regular classrooms. In other schools, important practical problems have been addressed, and new programs have been added to meet the special needs of some students. In some schools, little of significance has occurred. If student achievement is to improve measurably, more schools need to turn their attention to changing the ways in which regular students and teachers interact in the majority of the city's classrooms.

Vision and Accountability in School Improvement Planning

During the third year of reform, panel staff began intensive case studies of three schools that were moving to significantly alter their instructional programs (Flinspach and Ryan, 1992). As a part of this study, we reported on the development of LSCs in terms of their capacity to do concrete planning for school improvement. In reviewing the SIP revisions in our fourteen study schools, we found that different schools took different approaches, primarily depending on the type of leadership provided by the principal. It is the responsibility of the principal to present a SIP to the LSC for consideration, possible amendment, and adoption. The principal is to prepare the SIP in consultation with the LSC, the school staff, parents, and members of the local community. In just over one-half of our schools, the principals managed the SIP process but involved others, particularly teachers, in designing the proposed plans. In three schools, the SIPs were delegated to others to prepare. In a couple of our schools, principals developed and revised SIPs by themselves, sometimes soliciting input from teachers and others.

Either indirectly or directly, at most schools teachers had significant input into the development of their schools' SIPs during the third year of reform. They either composed core groups headed by the principals or participated in committees addressing different parts of the plans. Some grade-level meetings and department meetings were focused on SIP revision, and their recommendations were brought to the group compiling the plan. Schools varied widely in the degree of teacher involvement, but our interviews with teacher leaders in each school indicated that teachers have become progressively more involved in the planning process during the first three years of reform. These leaders indicated that early on, teachers were unwilling to commit extensive time and energy creating plans that they doubted would ever be implemented. However, as teachers found that components of earlier SIPs were being implemented, their attitudes began to change. By the third year, these leaders suggested, teachers generally believed that their voices would be heard and that their suggestions would be backed by the principals and would have adequate funding. This is an important development, given the literature on the crucial importance of teacher involvement in successful instructional innovation (McLaughlin, 1978; Elmore, 1978).

LSCs continue to be the governing bodies charged to adopt the SIPs. In eight of our schools, the LSCs took a formal role in preparing the draft SIPs; in the other six, the LSCs had no role until the draft plans were presented to them, which they then routinely adopted. Similarly, eight of the fourteen schools had conducted some monitoring and evaluation of the previous year's SIPs. In four of these schools, the monitoring was quite informal, with teachers discussing progress in staff meetings or the principals reporting achievements to the LSCs. Two schools formed monitoring committees, but one of these never met; the other did an end-of-year summative evaluation. The remaining two schools had more formal systems, giving regular updates to their LSCs. In one school, a self-evaluation instrument was used to gauge the extent of SIP implementation.

As we assessed the evaluation of the SIPs operative during 1991–92, it became obvious that in one-third of our sample schools the formally adopted SIPs had little effect on the regular, daily life of the schools. In these schools, the SIPs were rarely discussed by anyone; teachers were unaware of their contents; principals could not find copies of the plans. In most cases, these plans were not realistically related to the life of the schools. In another one-third of the schools, plans were occasionally discussed, but they were not a regular part of the life of the schools. In the remaining one-third of the schools, the SIPs played a much more vital role; they were regularly discussed in PPAC meetings, and teachers were actively engaged in revising the plans for 1992–93 implementation.

From our study of the fourteen SIPs, we found that some SIP initiatives (planned changes) were characterized by vague or generalized descriptions of existing practices, initiatives that sounded good but were unlikely to be implemented, or goal statements that were without implementation activities or programs. We called such initiatives *symbolic plans*. By contrast, we called initiatives planned by their implementors *pragmatic plans*, and we found that they were more likely to lead to school improvement. Improvement planning at two of the case study schools has become increasingly pragmatic over the last two years, and one case has been pragmatic during the entire reform period. A brief description of the planning process in two schools may make the distinction between symbolic and pragmatic plans clearer.

At a school we are calling Montgomery Elementary, the incumbent principal, obeying the mandate, though not the spirit, of the reform law, drew up the first SIP by himself. The plan included vague initiatives and perfunctory descriptions of routine operations such as "monitor instruction and pupil progress" and "organize school for instruction next year." He also included items that sounded good but were not meant to be implemented, such as "utilize computers and calculators in the instructional program" (though no computers were made available to teachers) and "evaluate pupil progress in all subject areas and adjust instruction to meet individual pupil needs as is necessary." His real attitude toward reform, however, was revealed in this passage from the plan: "School reform is a paper-intensive, meeting-oriented, time-consuming effort that diminished the energy and creative talents of the staff and parents who are sincerely attempting to meet the demands placed upon them. If legislative mandates are all that is needed to correct social conditions and shortcomings there would be no problems with drugs, crime, poverty or the myriad other problems facing society."

During the following year (1990–91), the Montgomery LSC was charged to evaluate the principal and decide on his retention or replacement. Two days before the second-year SIP had to be adopted, a new principal began her tenure. The outgoing principal had prepared the second-year SIP in the same way as he had the first. Too late to completely change the process, the new principal added three of her own initiatives, in response to concerns expressed by staff and parents: hiring another teacher to extend the kindergarten classes to a full-day program, devising an after-school program, and hiring a security guard. These three practical initiatives, characterized in our "Midway Report" (see Easton and others, 1991b) as add-on planning, were instituted at the beginning of the 1991–92 school year; the rest of the SIP was ignored as irrelevant.

During the third year of reform, these new initiatives were seen as significant improvements in the life of Montgomery. The full-day kindergarten was seen to be beneficial, as was the after-school program. The new security guard relieved the feeling of "unsafety" that has pervaded the school previously. More important, the man hired, a moonlighting Chicago policeman, saw his job as that of providing not only a sense of security in the school but also advice to students; he was actively engaged in the effort to improve Montgomery, interacted regularly with the principal, and was very responsive to requests for assistance from individual teachers. These add-on initiatives had created a climate in which more fundamental change could be undertaken.

When the new principal began the planning process for the SIP to be adopted in spring 1992, teachers were much more willing to participate. The principal chaired the ten-week process of developing the plan. She reviewed the record of student achievement in the school and the systemwide goals and objectives of reform adopted by the Chicago Board of Education. She gave a list of suggestions but also solicited input from the faculty members. The final plan presented to the LSC was prioritized to reflect the new funds available in the next year's school budget and was focused on the five subject areas included in the system's guide to improvement planning. It was full of very pragmatic plans. We called this type of planning *thematic*. In our opinion, it represents the first level of realistic planning for school improvement.

Further along in the SIP process is a school we are calling Winkle Elementary. During the first three years of school reform, Winkle introduced many new initiatives: Socratic seminars to improve the intellectual content of classroom discussion, extensive use of hands-on learning in mathematics, focus on experiments in science, and use of the Illinois Writing Project to implement a schoolwide writing emphasis. Teacher involvement in the planning process had been high in the 1990–91 and 1991–92 SIPs; teachers accepted the idea that they were accountable for plan implementation; they changed the means of instruction for writing, mathematics, and science. Winkle was doing the kind of instructional improvement planning that we hoped other schools would emulate. Their planning reflected a vision of a renewed partnership between staff, students, and parents. We called this type of effort *directed planning*.

During the 1991–92 school year, with teachers struggling to incorporate these many changes, the principal decided it was time to shift the SIP focus from staff development to student development, the second leg of the three-sided partnership. In an effort to make upper-grade students "responsible for what they produce in school," the principal proposed the establishment of stiff minimum eighth-grade graduation requirements, combined with a revamping of the seventh and eighth grades ("junior high") into an ungraded, project-oriented, portfolio-assessed school within the larger school. From the teachers' standpoint, several of these initiatives needed reworking in order to be implemented. They thought of the principal's suggestions as a skeleton for improvement, and they viewed their job as that of mediating between these directed plans and their real-world classroom embodiments. They retained the existing grade structure and developed a structure of projects similar to that operative in the then-current year. By utilizing a more incremental approach to planning, rather than the more radical implementation of the shared vision of student responsibility originally proposed, the teachers accepted only the amount of instructional change with which they were comfortable. Together, the teachers and the principal negotiated the planned changes in the directed planning proposals, eventually adopting the high graduation standards and a project approach to curriculum. The principal, appreciating the crucial importance of staff consensus in the planning process to the maintenance of staff accountability, compromised on the implementation plan for the 1992–93 school year.

Based on the experiences of the fourteen schools in our qualitative study, we have devised a SIP model that draws significantly on the work of Louis and Miles (1990). On one side is symbolic planning, which is largely disconnected from reality, whether due to generalized statements, abstract goals without implementation plans, or "sound-good" initiatives disconnected from the school's realities. In our sample of schools, we found no significant school improvement resulting from symbolic initiatives. On the other side are initiatives characterized by two major types of pragmatic planning. Thematic initiatives introduce major new programs. Directed initiatives also consist of major innovations, but each is specifically designed to make progress toward fulfillment of a shared school vision that emerged from the previous SIP efforts of the school community. To date, at least four of the fourteen schools we are studying are seriously engaged in pragmatic planning for their instructional programs. Only one of the four, Winkle Elementary, has reached the point of having a shared vision, and it is the only school in our sample that has attempted directed planning. If school reform is to be effective in Chicago, more of the system's 540 schools must attend to the job of thematic and directed planning to improve their instructional programs for the city's students.

Our monitoring and evaluation of the school restructuring effort in Chicago are in part designed to keep researchers across the country abreast of ongoing developments in this most radical of school reform efforts. Far more important, our work is designed to keep LSC members, school staffs, parents of students, community residents, and the area's policymakers informed on the current status of the reform efforts and on the direction that we think reform must take in the years ahead if the city's students are to be educated at a more adequate level than has been achieved in the past.

References

Bryk, A. S., and Raudenbush, S. *Hierarchical Linear Models for Social and Behavioral Research: Applications and Data Analysis Methods.* Newbury Park, Calif.: Sage, 1992.

Dean, P., Bryk, A. S., and Easton, J. Q. "Studying School Improvement in Chicago: A Construction of Post-Reform School Index Measures." Paper presented at the annual meeting of the American Educational Research Association, San Francisco, April 1992.

Easton, J. Q. *Teacher Attitudes Toward School Reform*. Chicago: Chicago Panel on Public School Policy and Finance, 1989.

Easton, J. Q., Dean, P., and Bryk, A. S. "School Change and Its Correlates: Studying Chicago Public Elementary Schools After School Reform." Paper presented at the annual meeting of the American Educational Research Association, San Francisco, April 1992.

Easton, J. Q., and Storey, S. L. *Attendance in Chicago Public Schools*. Chicago: Chicago Panel on Public School Policy and Finance, 1990a.

Easton, J. Q., and Storey, S. L. *Local School Council Meetings During the First Year of Chicago School Reform*. Chicago: Chicago Panel on Public School Policy and Finance, 1990b.

Easton, J. Q., and others. *Charting Reform: The Teachers' Turn*. Chicago: Consortium on Chicago School Research, 1991a.

Easton, J. Q., and others. *Decision Making and School Improvement: LSCs in the First Two Years of Reform*. Chicago: Chicago Panel on Public School Policy and Finance, 1991b.

Easton, J. Q., and others. *Research Summary and Self-Evaluation Guide: LSCs in the First Two Years of Reform*. Chicago: Chicago Panel on Public School Policy and Finance, 1992.

Elmore, R. F. "Organizational Models of Social Program Implementation." In D. Mann (ed.), *Making Change Happen*. New York: Teachers College Press, 1978.

Elmore, R. F. "Foreword." In G. Alfred Hess, Jr., *School Restructuring, Chicago Style*. Newbury Park, Calif.: Corwin Press, 1991.

Flinspach, S. L., and Ryan, S. P. *Vision and Accountability in School Improvement Planning*. Chicago: Chicago Panel on Public School Policy and Finance, 1992.

Ford, D. "The School Principal and Chicago School Reform." Paper presented at the annual meeting of the American Educational Research Association, San Francisco, April 1992.

Habermas, J. *Knowledge and Human Interest*. (Jeremey J. Shapiro, trans.) Boston: Beacon Press, 1971.

Habermas, J. *Theory and Practice*. (John Viertel, trans.) Boston: Beacon Press, 1978.

Harris, M. *America Now: The Anthropology of a Changing Culture*. New York: Simon & Schuster, 1981.

Hess, G. A., Jr. "School Reform in Chicago: Where's the Reality?" *Illinois Schools Journal*, 1991, 71 (1), 10–17.

Hess, G. A., Jr. "Anthropology and School Reform: To Catalog or Critique?" *Anthropology and Education Quarterly*, 1992a, 23 (3), 175–184.

Hess, G. A., Jr. "Chicago and Britain: Experiments in Empowering Parents." *Journal of Education Policy*, 1992b, 7 (2), 155–171.

Hess, G. A., Jr. "Midway Through School Reform in Chicago." *International Journal of Educational Reform*, 1992c, 1 (3), 270–284.

Hess, G. A., Jr. "Restructuring the Chicago Public Schools." In C. E. Finn, Jr., and T. Rebarber (eds.), *Education Reform in the '90s*. New York: Macmillan, 1992d.

Hess, G. A., Jr. *Restructuring Schools, Chicago Style: A Midway Report*. Chicago: Chicago Panel on Public School Policy and Finance, 1992e.

Hess, G. A., Jr., and Easton, J. Q. "Who's Making What Decisions?: Monitoring Authority Shifts in Chicago School Reform." In G. A. Hess, Jr. (ed.), *Empowering Teachers and Parents: School Restructuring Through the Eyes of Anthropologists*. Westport, Conn.: Bergin & Garvey, 1992.

Hess, G. A., Jr., and Lauber, D. *Dropouts from the Chicago Public Schools*. Chicago: Chicago Panel on Public School Finances, 1985.

Hess, G. A., Jr., and others. " 'Where's Room 185?' How Schools Can Reduce Their Dropout Problem." *Education and Urban Society*, 1987, 19 (3), 330–355.

Holland, D. C., and Eisenhart, M. A. *Educated in Romance: Women, Achievement, and College Culture*. Chicago: University of Chicago Press, 1990.

Louis, K. S., and Miles, M. *Improving the Urban High School: What Works and Why.* New York: Teachers College Press, 1990.

McLaughlin, M. W. "Implementation as Mutual Adaptation: Change in Classroom Organization." In D. Mann (ed.), *Making Change Happen.* New York: Teachers College Press, 1978.

Marcus, G. E., and Fischer, M. *Anthropology as Cultural Critique.* Chicago: University of Chicago Press, 1986.

Ogbu, J. *Minority Education and Caste: The American System in Cross-Cultural Perspective.* San Diego: Academic Press, 1978.

Ryan, S. P. "School Improvement Plan Implementation and Instructional Change." Paper presented at the annual meeting of the American Educational Research Association, San Francisco, April 1992.

G. ALFRED HESS, JR., is executive director of the Chicago Panel on Public School Policy and Finance, a nonprofit coalition of twenty agencies in Chicago dedicated to improving the Chicago public schools.

SUSAN LEIGH FLINSPACH and SUSAN P. RYAN are research analysts for the Chicago panel.

This chapter examines special education practices within Chicago school reform.

"And We Will Welcome Them": Reforming Special Education Through Chicago School Reform

Thomas Hehir

A local school council (LSC) had sent a letter to the Chicago Board of Education (CBE) claiming that the Department of Special Education was engaged in "top-down decision making" by requiring the principal to develop services for students with disabilities living in the attendance area. According to the district superintendent, the school had historically resisted housing special education and, contrary to the principal's claim, the school had more than sufficient space to house these services. The central administration office was willing to fund additional support staff to serve the students, and there was considerable advocacy pressure on behalf of the students. The issue came to a head when central office staff attended a special meeting of the LSC to resolve the problem.

The meeting began with considerable tension in the air as I, the associate superintendent at that time, explained why I had ordered the school to serve students with disabilities. I asserted that all schools in the city were required to serve students with disabilities within their attendance areas for whom such placements were deemed appropriate. Further, I stated that the goal of the system was to serve all students with disabilities in the least-restrictive environment—that is, disabled students would be served as much as possible with nondisabled students—a concept that is incorporated in federal law and increasingly recognized as educationally appropriate for most students with disabilities (Biklen, 1985). After I explained that Chicago had historically segregated large numbers of students with disabilities and that such practices were potentially harmful, a discussion ensued about inclusion of students with disabilities within their community schools. A LSC member inquired about whether there were other students with more substantial disabilities residing in the attendance area: "What about students they call TMH?" (The reference was to *trainable mentally handicapped*, a somewhat pejorative term still used in Illinois to describe students with moderate to severe cognitive delays.) I explained that there were five such students who resided in the school's attendance area and that all of them were being served elsewhere. After stating the department's policy to not move students against their parents' will, I stated my belief that in all likelihood, given the increased momentum among parents around the issue of inclusion, it would not be long before a parent of a child with a severe disability would be seeking admission to the school. Another LSC member interjected, "And we will welcome them."

Shortly after the meeting, the children involved in the dispute were admitted and granted special education services. What the central bureaucracy had failed to accomplish for years, the development of services for students with disabilities in this school, was accomplished in one LSC meeting. This is more than just a story of how school reform has worked to improve options for students with disabilities in one school in Chicago. It is also a metaphor of how systemic change is happening throughout the city as special education reform is progressing within the context of Chicago school reform, "top-down and bottom-up."

Context of Special Education Prior to Reform

Special education in Chicago, as in many large cities, was plagued with serious problems prior to school reform and, like many of its urban counterparts, was subject to class-action litigation. In 1982, Designs for Change, an educational advocacy group, published a report that documented a strong pattern of disproportionate placement of African American students in Chicago's programs for the *educable mentally handicapped* (another pejorative term, referring to students with mild mental retardation or cognitive delay). The Chicago Public School (CPS) System, at the direction of the then-superintendent Ruth Love, responded to the report by reevaluating all students placed in these classes and removing those who had been inappropriately placed. The U.S. Office of Civil Rights (OCR), prompted by numerous complaints from parents and advocates, took action against the district in 1986 for failure to conduct special education evaluations in a timely manner and for failure to place students in special education programs once evaluated. At the time of the administrative hearing in 1987, only 18 percent of the evaluations were conducted on time and over 1,891 children waited over a year for their evaluations to be completed. It was estimated that 300 students were unplaced. The judge was so appalled with the condition of special education that he referred to "special education perversities in Chicago" in his decision. Faced with a loss of up to $100 million in federal funds for failure to implement federal special education law, CBE entered into a settlement agreement requiring, among other things, that it reorganize its special education program and take necessary steps to ensure 100 percent compliance with the law. The Illinois State Board of Education (ISBE) took similar action over Chicago's failure to implement state special education law, resulting in the generation of a similar consent agreement that required CBE to also address the underrepresentation of Hispanics, as well as the overrepresentation of African Americans, in special education programs.

Additional class actions occurred during the late 1980s. One, *Calvin G.*, involved the failure of CBE to provide speech services to students with severe hearing loss, and another, *Katie I.*, involved the failure to serve wards of the state. In *Calvin G.*, it was alleged that CBE had categorically denied speech services to deaf students in direct violation of state and federal laws. The Cook County Public Guardian, representing the plaintiffs in *Katie I.*, documented that students with disabilities who were wards of the state were denied equal education by being confined to separate "shelter classrooms" and that many of these students were labeled as disabled without a special education evaluation simply because they were wards or because they were incarcerated. Additional consent agreements resulted from both of these cases.

Special Education Reorganization

The initial implementation of the OCR consent agreement and the Chicago School Reform Act of 1988 coincided, and given the strong role that special education advocates had played in the reform movement, it was not surprising that the OCR agreement incorporated many of the principles of the overall reform movement. Some reformers believed that many of the problems of special education were the result of a cumbersome and unwieldy centralized system. The OCR agreement called for considerable decentralization. The central and district offices were cut from approximately 480 professional positions to 145. Most assessors were to be distributed to school units and were to be accountable to the principals of those schools. The agreement also called for the establishment of an associate superintendent for special education and pupil support services, who would report to the general superintendent. The authors of the consent agreement recognized that decentralization of special education to the principals would not in itself safeguard the rights of students with disabilities. The agreement provided that the associate superintendent would have the authority to order principals to take action necessary to comply with laws related to the education of students with disabilities. CBE was further required to conduct a national search for the associate super-intendent candidates and to meet hiring goals for various special education personnel.

During the first year of the implementation of the consent agreement, the position of associate superintendent was filled on an interim basis by an able and popular "insider," Barbara Williams. She oversaw the decen-tralization of assessment staff to the schools and began the task of imple-menting the consent agreement. In 1990, Williams made a decision, which may have seemed routine at the time, that had a significant long-term impact on special education. She resolved an OCR complaint in favor of a parent who was seeking the enrollment of her son with severe disabilities in the same school that his sisters attended. Although the school was physically accessible and her son, Joe, was gifted intellectually, the parent, Mrs. Ford, discovered that the school was hardly barrier-free. She was told by CBE officials that Joe could not attend the school because he had a severe physical disability and used a wheelchair. Fortunately, this parent knew her child's rights and would not accept this exclusion. She knew that Joe's placement in a segregated environment would be detrimental to his educational and social development. Away from his sisters and friends from the neighborhood, he would not have contact with children who did not have disabilities. Aware that children with disabilities were guaranteed by federal and state laws the right to be educated as much as possible with their nondisabled peers, she filed a complaint with OCR. After her many hours of effort on Joe's behalf, he enrolled in the first grade in September 1990.

Although the system was under four consent agreements regarding special education, none of these had dealt specifically with the issue that Joe's case dramatized, the pervasive segregation of students with disabili-ties. Chicago had routinely segregated most of its students with moderate to severe disabilities, and many with mild disabilities. Contrary to federal and state laws, students were placed in special education based solely on their categories and levels of disability. The system of serving students with disabilities reflected the previous centralized structure of special educa-tion. The central department had been organized around the various disability areas, with each disability having its own directors, staff, pro-grams, and, in some cases, schools. The central bureaucracy had done what bureaucracies do best—routine tasks. Students, when they finally got evaluated, were sorted by category and level of disability and placed in programs accordingly. Therefore, Joe, who had severe physical disabilities, was treated by the bureaucracy like all other children with severe disabili-ties; he was placed in a special school run by the central bureaucracy.

Although this practice might be characterized as typical organizational behavior of a bureaucracy, it departed significantly from federal and state statutes requiring individualized placements in the least restrictive environment, as close as possible to nondisabled students. When Joe's mother challenged his placement, the bureaucracy initially fought back. Joe was a threat to the centralized system of special education, to a powerful status quo. If Joe was allowed to enroll in the first grade, many others might follow. Would there be a need for segregated schools and the categorical central departments that ran them if this one outcome started a trend?

Joe's case could not have come at a better time. When Mrs. Ford was challenging the placement of her son, Chicago school reform was challenging the power of the central bureaucracy and calling for it to be downscaled. Joe's case added an important issue to the mix: inclusion. It raised the question of how students with disabilities were to be included in the overall movement to reform education in the city. Joe became the "poster child" of what has developed into a powerful movement in Chicago to enroll students with disabilities in their local schools, to define children with disabilities in the school reform movement. The organizational assumptions on which Chicago's school reform movement was based challenged the very foundation of the centralized bureaucracy: the need to "run" education from a central office. The sheer inability of the large central special education department to implement the basic requirements of special education law provided concrete support to a basic organizational assumption of the reform movement: School systems are loosely coupled organizations (Weick, 1976).

The reform movement recognized that schools, not school systems, educate children. The school reform act incorporated this important principle in the legislation, calling for greater discretion and responsibility at the school site level. The legislation also recognized another key concept needed to improve schools (Comer, 1987; Edmonds, 1979): community involvement. Mrs. Ford was seeking to have Joe educated with others within his community, and she successfully wrested the control of her son's education away from the central bureaucracy. In so doing, she further dramatized the need for students with disabilities to be defined within their communities as school reform progressed. Chicago school reform thus presented an unprecedented opportunity to reform special education.

Special Education Reform

When I was appointed associate superintendent for special education and pupil support services in August 1990, the initial phases of reorganization had been completed; the central office had been downsized and most direct service staff had been deployed to school units. However, there was still much that remained to be done. There was a backlog of over five thousand students who required evaluations, and there were twenty-four hundred unplaced students. Further, though much of the decentralization had taken place, the remaining central structure had significant overlaps and did not support the overall goal of reform: the development of more effective schools. Most disturbing, however, was the continuation of a centralized placement system in special education that reflected the previous organizational structure of the department; students were still being placed on the basis of their disability categories and the severity of those disabilities and, for students in most disability categories, those placements were not in their home communities. Further, these students had limited access to magnet programs.

In September 1990, the Department of Special Education and Pupil Support Services established three goals, which remain in effect: to comply with law pertaining to the education of students with disabilities, to serve students with disabilities as much as possible in the schools they would have attended were they not disabled, and to include students with disabilities as much as possible with their nondisabled peers. The department also redefined its role, shifting from the "running" of special education to a support and monitoring function. The department's functions are essentially to help the local schools improve their services to students with disabilities and to monitor the provision of services to students with disabilities.

To support these goals and improve efficiency, the department established district teams of generic special education and pupil support services administrators. These teams of three administrators for each of the ten elementary school subdistricts and one team of eight for the high schools support the principals and LSCs in developing services for students with disabilities and in improving their overall pupil support services.

After approximately two and one-half years under this structure, there has been notable progress in achieving the goals of the department. The following is a summary of the improvements in serving students with disabilities within the context of Chicago school reform.

Compliance

Although CPSs have not achieved the 100 percent compliance level called for in the OCR agreement, major strides have been made. During the 1991–92 school year, the district achieved a 60 percent timeliness record on evaluations and, for the first time, virtually eliminated its evaluation backlog. Further, it should be noted that when the administrative law judge heard the OCR case, 5,083 students waited for over 180 days for an evaluation. Last year, 76 students waited that long, and in most of these cases the reasons for delay were beyond the control of the CPSs. This school year, given the absence of the backlog and improved monitoring, we expect to achieve an 80 percent level of compliance with the timeliness requirement.

The decentralization of special education evaluation services has resulted in much higher levels of compliance than achieved by the previously centralized system, and continued improvements can be expected. However, though major progress has been made, current levels of compliance are not good enough. The overall level of compliance reflects the cumulative performance of 600 schools, and the performance of individual schools varies widely. There are over 170 schools in Chicago that performed above the 80 percent level, while 83 failed to reach 40 percent. In some cases, the failure to comply with timeliness standards was beyond the control of the schools due to the lack of availability of critical assessors—most typically, speech therapists. However, most schools with timeliness problems have sufficient resources to conduct their meetings on time. The practice of simply redistributing staff to schools has not guaranteed compliance. Monitoring and intervention are needed at the school level to ensure that students with disabilities receive appropriate protection. In cases where schools have demonstrated a pattern of failing to conduct their meetings on time, they are now each required to develop a corrective action plan with the district team.

In the area of placement, there are currently forty-eight students who require a special education program but have not been placed. The elimination of the large placement backlog has been greatly enhanced by our movement to home school placement. We have required that all schools build service delivery capacity so that, at minimum, students with mild to moderate disabilities can be served in their home schools. Further, when parents of children with more severe disabilities want their children to be served in home schools, the central office works with the schools to develop options.

Over the past two decades, we in special education have learned that most students with disabilities can be provided with services in their home schools and communities. We have moved away from the notion that special education is a place to a reconceptualization of special education as individualized services tailored to the child with the goal of full participation in the school and the community. Although full achievement of this ideal will require much work over the coming years, notable progress has occurred.

Currently, over thirty thousand of the district's forty-four thousand students with disabilities are being served in their home schools or in magnet options. That compares with under sixteen thousand students two years ago. The previous practice of sending students away from their home schools to receive special education services is diminishing at a rate that has far exceeded my expectation. Although we required all schools to develop services, we had aimed at a final implementation date of September 1993. The goal has largely been achieved a year ahead of time due to the strong support that the concept of home school placement has received from parents of students with disabilities, principals, and LSC members. There are many parents like Mrs. Ford who do not want their children bused to distant schools away from their brothers and sisters and friends. They do not want to have to interact with schools far removed from their homes and communities. Also, most principals have responded favorably to the premise that all principals have equal responsibility. Many reported to me that they had no trouble with the idea of serving "their own kids." The positive response of the LSC in the opening story of this chapter is not unique. Given the strong emphasis on the concept of community in Chicago school reform efforts, the inclusion of people with disabilities is compelling. Finally, many parents of children with disabilities serve on LSCs as well as some adults with disabilities. Such participation in the governance of school affairs, through the LSC, has generally had a positive impact on the education of students with disabilities.

Inclusion

The movement of students with disabilities to home schools is generally a requirement for successful inclusion but not a guarantee that it will occur. Students with disabilities can be segregated in any environment. Although there has been significant movement toward more inclusive approaches, progress has not been as rapid in this area as it has been in compliance-oriented matters. This difference probably reflects the degree of complexity and difficulty inherent to the task of moving a system from traditional categorical segregation to inclusive education. Successful inclusion requires both technical and cultural changes in schooling. Technical change refers to the way in which instruction provided to disabled students in inclusive environments is different from that provided in segregated environments. Individualized planning, cooperative teaching, cooperative learning, and community-based instruction are all necessary components of inclusive education, which take time to develop. The primary cultural change that must occur is the acceptance of the value that *all children* have a right to fully participate in all aspects of their school's life. That change in values takes time as well.

In our efforts to foster a greater degree of inclusion for students with disabilities, we have emphasized the importance of having schools develop their own approaches to inclusion. Toward that end, we have supported schools willing to serve as model sites for inclusion with small inclusion grants of $5,000, and these schools have been provided with technical assistance from both central office and ISBE staff. Schools that agree to become inclusive school demonstration sites respond to a "request for proposals" (RFP) and must agree to enroll students with all levels of severity of disabilities. Each school is required to establish an advisory committee including both regular and special educators, and all proposals must be endorsed by the LSC. Over sixty schools have responded to the RFP, and many have developed unique and innovative approaches. These bottom-up inclusion initiatives received the highest level of top-down support when Mayor Richard Daley declared November 4–8, 1991, "Inclusive Schools Week."

In addition to these initiatives by the local schools, most of the seventeen public special education schools have taken steps to desegregate and to increase the number of options for their students to be included. Seven of these schools have begun reverse integration programs, enrolling nondisabled students. Others are working with local schools to develop options for their students to be included. The city has approved plans to expand two of the early childhood special education centers into comprehensive early childhood centers for both disabled and nondisabled students. In both cases, the LSCs of these schools effectively lobbied officials (including myself) to provide the resources necessary to integrate these centers.

In addition to the generally positive response of many school communities toward more inclusive approaches, individual parents continue to serve as catalysts on behalf of students with disabilities within their local schools. One by one, parents of students with moderate to severe disabilities are petitioning their local schools for admittance and appropriate support services once enrolled. Sometimes these parents require the help of the central office in securing these placements, and we assist them on a one-to-one basis. However, in many instances the local schools respond without the intervention of the central office.

Recently, I was visiting a school in which I noticed a child with Down syndrome included in a kindergarten class. The girl was considered to have moderate cognitive delay and, under traditional special education practices, would have been placed in the TMH class, probably in another school. I asked the principal how she had become enrolled in the kindergarten at her neighborhood school. She replied that the little girl's father had sought enrollment of his daughter in the school and that the special education staff had met and saw no reason why she could not be included. In this school, there was no need for central involvement in the placement of this student; the school simply provided appropriate services and access for the student. And, most important, the central office no longer had either the inclination or the power to remove the student from her community. Her father had thankfully been spared Mrs. Ford's ordeal.

Future Opportunities and Concerns

The experience of the first three years of Chicago school reform implementation has demonstrated that the opportunity presented for reform of special education has indeed become a promising reality for many children and parents. There has been marked progress in many areas, though much remains to be done. The progress of individual schools in their ability to serve students with disabilities varies considerably, as expected in a decentralized system. (Of course, there is variability in centralized systems as well.) True reform for students with disabilities occurs on a school-by-school basis. The central challenge, therefore, is to build the capacity of each CPS to serve students with disabilities.

Development of this capacity of individual schools must begin with an unqualified recognition that students with disabilities have rights to access effective education with appropriate support. No LSC, principal, central administrator, or teacher can legally deny those rights. Schools, therefore, must develop their capacity to serve students with disabilities. CBE has a responsibility to protect those rights, and the central special education department has to take a hard line with schools that do not adhere to the civil rights of students with disabilities. As my opening story illustrates, some schools have resisted this assertion of central authority. However, these schools are relatively few in number.

CPSs can be roughly divided into three categories: (1) those with excellent services in which children with disabilities are included and regulatory compliance is high, (2) those that have yet to fully develop their support systems and are not fully compliant but are sincerely interested in improving, and (3) those that continue to resist serving students with disabilities. The greatest number of schools fall into the second category. A significant and growing number of schools fall into the first category, while a smaller number fall into the third. Schools in the first category are obviously the ideal, and the system's goal is to move all schools into that category. If that were the case throughout the system, there would be relatively little need for a central department of special education. The schools would only need support in the schools in order to maintain their success. However, given that most of our schools have not achieved the ideal, there continues to be a need for central oversight and support. Schools that have not yet fully developed their support systems require assistance in improving their programmatic options and must be monitored to ensure compliance. Recalcitrant schools need a significant amount of enforcement pressure.

My greatest concern (which may sound more like self-interest to some) is whether there will continue to be a sufficient central presence in special education to ensure continued progress given the widespread disregard within Chicago for the central office. A convenient scapegoat for the ills of the system, the call goes out every year during our annual budget crisis to cut central office personnel and services. Even though the central office has been cut well below the level specified in the reform act, in the summer of 1991 the School Finance Authority issued a focus report recommending the complete elimination of some central departments, including special education. The report advocated that special education administration functions be assumed by state and federal government agencies. There was no analysis of whether the state or the federal government had either the person power or the capacity to monitor six hundred schools in a system with deep and long-standing compliance and service delivery problems. (The federal government's Office of Special Education Programs has one compliance officer assigned to Illinois, who also covers other states as well.) Nonetheless, the finance authority forwarded the report to CBE and pressured board members for a response. CBE made an across-the-board cut in the central office, with the special education department experiencing one of the deepest cuts, 20 percent.

Fortunately, the staff that is left is highly dedicated and works long hours. However, some very capable staff have left the central office seeking less demanding and more secure jobs. If the department experiences another severe cutback, the prospect for continued improvement is unlikely.

Overall, the initial report card on how reform has impacted special education is indeed positive. Accountability and resources for educating students with disabilities are where they should be, at the school sites within the communities in which we want to see these children included. There is, however, much to do, and continued progress is threatened unless there is a recognition that the strategy of simply giving schools resources and responsibility is no guarantee that the rights of students with disabilities will be respected. It would be a tragedy if the unique opportunity presented by Chicago school reform is sacrificed on the altar of reform extremists in their apparent headlong assault on all that is associated with the central office. The early experience of school reform shows that at least in the area of special education, where the needs of students have been neglected for so long, the best course continues to be top-down, bottom-up.

References

Biklen, D. *Achieving the Complete School: Strategies for Effective Mainstreaming.* New York: Teachers College Press, 1985.

Comer, J. "New Haven's School-Community Curriculum." *Educational Leadership,* 1987, *44* (6).

Edmonds, R. "Effective Schools for the Urban Poor." *Educational Leadership,* 1979, *37,* 15–27.

Weick, E. "Educational Organizations as Loosely Coupled Systems." *Administrative Science Quarterly,* 1976, *21* (1).

THOMAS HEHIR is former associate superintendent for special education and pupil support services in the Chicago public schools. He is currently senior researcher at the Education Development Center in Newton, Massachusetts.

How well do market pressures contribute to school improvement in high schools of choice? This chapter evaluates the relation between markets and reform by comparing two Catholic and two public high schools in Chicago.

School Improvement Processes: A Comparative Study of Chicago High Schools

James G. Cibulka

Neither the change nor the restructuring literature has paid much attention to market competition as a reform strategy. Competition, according to advocates such as Chubb and Moe (1990), leads to improved school performance, but no one has yet explained how this process of self-renewal occurs.

Research on public-private school comparisons, such as Coleman and Hoffer (1987) and Haertel, James, and Levin (1987), has documented that Catholic high schools have different characteristics from public ones, for example, clearer goals and less tracking. Whether these organizational differences lead to different student outcomes is disputed. What this literature does not document is how Catholic schools actually respond to pressures for change under conditions of market competitiveness.

Also unexamined in the reform literature is how public high schools of choice respond to market pressures. Accordingly, this chapter is a comparative case analysis of two Catholic high schools and two public high schools of choice, all located in Chicago.

This study differs from the research of Moore and Davenport (1990) and Wong (1992), who examined the externalities (indirect consequences) of choice arrangements in the Chicago public schools and concluded that choice programs increased inequality among schools. My purpose here, working from comparisons between Catholic and public high schools, is to document whether and how market competition spurs school improvement and reform. (A brief summary of the field methods is provided in the chapter Appendix.)

New Directions for Program Evaluation, no. 59, Fall 1993 © Jossey-Bass Publishers

Loss of Markets in Two Catholic High Schools

Both of the Catholic schools were selected for study because they serve mainly youth of color who live in the inner city. Both schools are located on Chicago's South Side in neighborhoods characterized by poverty, high crime, and violence. As a result of changes in their neighborhoods, as well as other factors, both schools have confronted severe external challenges. They were threatened with the loss of their traditional student body (market) and were impelled to respond. How they chose to respond, or, stated differently, how they interpreted their opportunities and constraints, is a study in sharp contrasts.

Academy of Our Lady. This girl's high school once served the social elite of Chicago's South Side. Its location on South Ninety-Fifth Street, not far from the Dan Ryan Expressway, had at one time been a major asset; this was a prosperous commercial thoroughfare, and its surrounding residential neighborhood, while not luxurious, was one of neat, well-kept houses. Academy of Our Lady enjoyed a large facility on ample grounds adjacent to the convent where the Dominican sisters lived.

In the 1960s, this area underwent racial and, equally important, socioeconomic changes. According to one sister who witnessed the transition, the Chicago archdiocese decided that there would be no policy attempting to stem or manage this process. Thus, as the neighborhood became predominantly African American and much poorer, the school lost Caucasian students. Its total enrollment declined steadily, aggravated by generally low enrollments in both public and Catholic schools during this period due to a decline in the school-age population. Further, a new all-girl high school was built in a nearby suburb to serve Catholic families who had moved out of the city. Despite some recruitment efforts by Academy of Our Lady officials, this process of decline continued into the 1980s, and it became apparent that unless the trend could be reversed, the school might eventually be forced to close. While the administration of the school remained firmly in the hands of the sisters, the majority of the staff shifted from religious personnel to laypersons.

Upon the retirement of the long-standing principal, who was a Dominican sister, the schools' leadership was assumed by an African American woman. The previous administration of the school had represented a link with the past. A new leader might well change course. Yet the constraints proved formidable.

The cultivation of "ladies" had once been a strong goal at the school. The religious officials who sponsored the school remained committed to this special mission, even as they recognized the need to update the goals to fit a new clientele and a new era. Newer staff members had no such clear vision, either retrospective or prospective. In addition, poor salaries led to high staff turnover among the lay faculty, further contributing to the difficulties.

The problems were not lost on the girls attending the school. Many who were interviewed expressed frustration with what they interpreted as the overly strict, censorious atmosphere of the school. To this they added that the teaching staff, particularly the lay faculty, were of uneven quality. Parents echoed this concern. The school's reputation for safety was marred by a shooting at the night school conducted on the school's premises.

The school could not decide whether to maintain its college-oriented curriculum. While it officially retained its strong academic focus, the school's administration developed additional tracks to accommodate those who did not fit this academic ideal. Admissions standards were slackened over the years in an effort to overcome enrollment problems. Eventually, some students were admitted who were defined as remedial, with the intent that after one year they could be brought up to the performance level of other girls in the school. Because this goal was not achievable, at least in the short term, the school decided to abandon this more liberal admissions policy, returning instead to its traditional admissions standards and tracking.

The school's enrollments remained perilously low and its financial situation precarious. With respect to the latter, because of the low income level of many of the girls attending the school, financial assistance was required. Yet, the school's resources were extremely limited in this regard, and it depended on modest scholarship funds made available by the archdiocese. In short, by the early 1990s, no easy way out of the school's dilemmas had been discovered. The school seemed trapped by limited options—no longer in a desirable location; upstaged by a newer competitor serving a more affluent clientele in a superior, more modern facility; paralyzed by internal inertia as to mission and program redefinition; and caught in an image problem with students, parents, and the larger community that it could not readily resolve.

Saint Joseph High School. At one time this had been a small parish high school of approximately five hundred pupils serving a population of predominantly Polish and Eastern European heritage. The high school is immediately adjacent to the church, which is situated in a neighborhood of modest bungalows. The facility, which is very neatly kept and reflects a modernization in recent decades, has a cramped feeling. The library, for instance, is small, and there is no gymnasium.

At one time, the neighborhood had been solidly blue-collar. Fathers of the boys and girls attending the school had worked in the meat-packing houses near the Back-of-the-Yards community. Not only had the economic base of the community changed but also its racial makeup. In the 1970s, the neighborhood became predominantly Mexican American.

As the traditional membership of the parish grew older and moved, the school, while officially owned by the parish, became more of a burden than an asset. There were few resources in the small parish to subsidize a school, and the parish priest was known to be somewhat indifferent concerning whether the school should remain open. The school came to depend on subsidies from archdiocesan officials, who acquired more influence over the school's future.

The school's enrollments continued to diminish in the 1980s due to a reputation for violence and drugs in the neighborhood and in the school. Gangs were known to operate in the school, and a highly publicized stabbing had a traumatic impact on all associated with the school. Officials at other parishes in this part of the city declined to recommend the school to eighth graders attending catechism classes, and school officials were sometimes denied an opportunity to recruit at Catholic elementary schools. When a new principal was hired by the priest, this sister decided to change the image of the school. She began to visit classrooms regularly, refused to rehire teachers of whom she disapproved, instituted a strict policy prohibiting weapons or gang activity, set up a detention system, and attempted to create a close-knit, familylike atmosphere. Further, the school came to be marketed as a place for "second-chance" youngsters who had flunked at other Catholic schools or who found public schools too violent or permissive. Students who were admitted under these conditions were required to sign a written contract with their parents, and those failing to comply were given severe warnings, punishments, or dismissals.

This "tough love" policy, which eventually pervaded almost every aspect of the small school, was received positively by most students, albeit with considerable ambivalence. "We cannot get away with anything," they complained. The heavy monetary fines for tardiness or other infractions were regarded as unduly strict, even mercenary. However, all students felt cared for and were made to feel that they must do their best. "They won't let you goof off or make excuses, so I learned to respect myself and others. This has made a big difference for me," was a typical comment. The principal instituted a counseling program to deal with drug issues and teenage identity problems.

Teachers sometimes complain that the students are not as highly motivated as they would like and that the school does not get "the best pick," but as a result of the principal's leadership, staff embrace the philosophy that every student is important and must be treated with dignity so that they develop to their full potential. This developmental view, and the school's small size, led to a decision that the school would have only minimal tracking. All students are expected to perform in a college-oriented curriculum, which also emphasizes some job skills. According to many staff members, despite the strict rules most students are "babied" a lot, as they would be in nurturing families.

Although these leadership efforts by the principal turned around the reputation of the school and brought its enrollments up into the three hundreds, the size of the school remained perilously small, particularly in view of the dependence on archdiocesan scholarships for so many pupils. Archdiocesan support for inner-city parish schools grew increasingly uncertain in the 1990s, with announcements that many would be allowed to close rather than remain subsidized indefinitely. Further, the absence of Spanish-speaking staff members has limited the school's ability to create a strong bond with parents. Indeed, school officials feel a strong tension between the school's aspirations for girls to pursue post–high school education and the families' desires (particularly those of the fathers) that their daughters stay at home or get married. While these remain serious problems that cast a shadow over the school's future, the school had at least found a new mission and redesigned its culture and programs to reflect that mission, thus attracting for a time a new market that may guarantee its survival.

The Two Cases Compared: Response to Loss of a Market. Both of these Catholic schools struggled with how to respond appropriately to changes in their environments. The transition from a predominantly white clientele to one of color, and from a relatively affluent group (or, in the case of Saint Joseph, a working-class student body) to one that is predominantly poor, took place gradually. These schools did little to anticipate or steer the changes but instead responded belatedly. In this time frame, they did respond somewhat differently. Academy of Our Lady tried better publicity and a relaxation of admissions standards, but little else was done. Saint Joseph went much further in changing the stated mission of the school, its targeted market, staffing, and organizational culture.

Markets in Public High Schools of Choice

In this section, a brief overview is provided of two public high schools that have choice programs. In each case, the decision by school authorities at the central office to define the institution as a specialty or magnet school was intended to solve a problem in the school's relationship to its environment. How this decision was reached, by whom, using what definitions of the "problem" are critical considerations, however, in assessing what role choice arrangements had at these schools in generating actual school improvement.

Curie Metropolitan High School. Curie is one of the largest high schools in the city, with over three thousand pupils. Located in a modern facility on the city's southwest side, the school was a bone of contention from the late 1960s when discussions arose over the need for a new high school in the area. Then-superintendent James Redmond had announced plans to build a series of educational parks around the city. Later renamed cultural education clusters, a term it was hoped (to no avail) would avoid the controversial concept of racial busing, these schools were nonetheless supposed to be racially integrated. Strong community opposition from white residents forestalled construction of these new schools for many years. When Curie eventually was built, this achievement was due largely to the resolve of the district superintendent, whose popularity helped sell the idea to a reluctant community. By reserving a large number of slots for local (white) resident students and by imposing admissions standards for magnet students from outside the area, local concerns were at least mollified.

Eventually, however, responding to federal government pressures for more desegregation in the city's schools, school officials expanded the magnet portion of the school and virtually eliminated admissions requirements. Also, a changing demography on Chicago's southwest side (an aging white population, white flight from the public schools, and an expanding Hispanic population) created a new clientele for the school even within the local attendance area. Due to this combination of factors, the school's Hispanic and black populations grew, and the desegregation quotas created one of the few remaining racially balanced schools in the city of Chicago.

While the school's principal viewed this integrated student body as an achievement, white residents and white business leaders in the local area strongly disapproved of the specialty school. The visible presence of so many black and brown faces in the local neighborhood seemed to confirm their worst fears. Yet the Archer Park community was not particularly well organized to resist school officials.

Curie Metropolitan High School served a small, increasingly isolated community. Its principal market came from outside its administratively defined attendance area, and while the school drew mainly from the southwest side, it successfully recruited students from throughout the city.

At one level, this new market seemed a visible example of how choice arrangements could be used to create a school with a focused mission and thereby act as an important lever for school improvement. Yet, beneath this surface, market arrangements had merely disguised, rather than resolved, many problems. The school was marketed to potential students with a promotional zeal that caused some staff members to raise ethical questions. Many students and their parents seemed unaware that career opportunities in the performing arts were relatively limited. School officials covered potential criticism on this point by pointing out that the performing arts were meant only to be an avocation for most young people. Since school officials were not permitted, due to a board of education policy, to screen on the basis of aptitude (this was a "nonselective magnet" school), this avocational emphasis was probably realistic for many youngsters. Indeed, it reflected quite accurately the limited interest of many students in the performing arts, despite the fact that these students and their families sought out Curie. But their reasons for attending Curie had little to do with its performing arts emphasis. The majority of applicants were motivated to attend Curie to avoid violence and poor educational quality at their own attendance area high schools. Thus, the failure to deliver a marketable career was not a burning issue with them, and they tolerated what amounted to some degree of marketing deception because their other needs were being met. Nonetheless, complaints emerged from many college-bound students that the performing arts track was so rigid that it left insufficient space for liberal arts courses required for college admission. Further, students wishing to transfer from one performing arts emphasis to another, for example, from music to theater, were not allowed to do so, which seemed at odds with the avocational emphasis purportedly driving the curriculum.

These issues were not resolved internally because of teaching staff rivalries among performing arts, liberal arts, and vocational subjects. The school's administration devoted great attention to promoting the school's image but could or would not resolve these internal problems. The principal's approach to managing the school was largely technical and bureaucratic in the best sense of those words. The principal lacked the full commitment of the staff; many continued to resent his unsuccessful attempt to transfer them when he had first helped to set up the performing arts specialty. He measured the school's quality by the size of its market and its successful avoidance of racial conflict, which had once plagued the school and had led to his predecessor's departure.

In short, Curie had found a successful market niche, largely through skilled, indeed opportunistic, strategies for capturing that market. Yet, the process of school improvement also had sharp delimitations. The school remained, like many urban high schools, large, impersonal, and bureaucratic for both students and faculty. The learning opportunities that it offered some were superb, for others woefully inadequate. Students who were seniors sensed the unfulfilled potential of the school and were quick to articulate both the school's positive attributes and its drawbacks.

Chicago High School for the Agricultural Sciences. Unlike the other three high schools already discussed, Chicago High School for the Agricultural Sciences (Ag School) illustrates a different point about school improvement processes. Ag School was created as a new school in 1985. It was not encumbered by decades of tradition. In the space of less than a decade, it began to acquire a reputation for excellence, which brought it favorable attention from the media, including a 1992 feature in the *New York Times*.

The motives for creating the school were political. The Chicago Board of Education was responding to federal pressure for improved student desegregation, as described earlier with respect to Curie Metropolitan. At the same time, school officials were receiving pressure from local residents in the Mount Greenwood community on the city's far southwest side. In order to meet its financial obligations under the School Finance Authority, the board had planned to sell a large tract of land that was the last working farm in the city. The chairman of the Chicago Board of Trade took an interest in the dispute, and the decision was made not only to save the land but to put it to educational use. A citywide magnet school dealing with agribusiness was planned, and a closed elementary school adjacent to the property was remodeled until a new school could be built. While the remodeling was under way, the school operated as an outpost of Morgan Park High School. Because of the influence of the new school's advisory council, the school board eventually appropriated funds for a new school and successfully lobbied for state funding support, at a time when no other building projects were being supported in Chicago.

Because of delays in approval and construction of a new facility, students and staff struggled to endure one of the most cramped and otherwise unsuitable high school facilities imaginable. Yet, this adversity appeared to create a bond of mutual sacrifice. Further, the selection of an entirely new staff by the first principal, some recruited from as far away as Wisconsin, made all personnel feel privileged. Working under the freedom to create and experiment with a new curriculum, yet constrained by limited classroom space, the staff decided on a common core curriculum for all students, and minimal tracking. Within a number of years, the staff made the decision to eliminate all tracking. Further, because the school phased in its student body, beginning with a freshman class of 120, the school evolved as an extended family. While some staff acknowledged that they thought the students were babied too much, this personal, caring atmosphere bore striking similarities to the kind of environment often found in private schools, such as Saint Joseph High School, discussed earlier. It was not uncommon for students to seek help and advice from staff members outside of class, a pattern of interaction that seemed to evolve from the close physical proximity between students and staff. Students complained that personal reputations were set quickly in the school, since word traveled fast down hall corridors, and they said that they thought twice about skipping—"Besides, there's no place to go."

To be sure, Ag School had its share of growing pains. Its administrative procedures were incomplete, and students complained of confusion. Discipline seemed oddly out of keeping with the principal's philosophy. The facility led to program limitations. Also, the school had trouble attracting white students because local residents, despite their original fight to create a new school, were more oriented to parochial schools and resistant to desegregation. Still, the developmental philosophy of the school's staff (carried out even more self-consciously by the school's second principal, who came from an elementary school background), combined with the facilities constraints under which the school labored, set in motion school improvement processes that made Ag School an effective urban high school.

Some would argue that the school's success depends at least in part on its ability to recruit students; even though Ag School is a nonselective magnet, students are interviewed and the school works actively to improve its applicant pool. The low poverty rate among the student body bears this out. Yet, the desegregation requirements cause the school to accept white students who would not otherwise be accepted in order to meet the board's guidelines for 15 percent white pupils. Thus, even amid market arrangements, there is diversity in the student body in terms of academic and social backgrounds, which contributes to the school's egalitarian culture.

Conclusion

For only two of the four schools discussed here can it be said that the school improvement processes triggered by market pressures led to a fundamental reconceptualization of how an urban high school should be structured. Saint Joseph High School, with its new focus on providing a "second chance" for youth, and Ag School, a small familylike school with common, yet high, standards, seem to meet this criterion. The other two schools, Academy of Our Lady and Curie Metropolitan High School, used choice arrangements for school improvement, and each succeeded to some extent, but in a manner that left major problems and challenges at the schools largely untouched.

What differences separate Saint Joseph and Ag School from the other two schools? The distinguishing mark of the first two seems to be that market reform led to a comprehensive rethinking of the schools' missions, programs, and climates so that equitable and quality learning opportunities became available to as many students in the schools as possible. In the other two schools, by contrast, school improvement was defined more narrowly and, therefore, did not lead to fundamental changes.

Market arrangements do not guarantee rational behavior by school officials, any more than rationality is to be found in regulation through political processes. The difference between the two forms of regulation, however, is that market firms generally experience negative consequences for failing to respond rationally to an important market problem, whereas nonmarket firms rarely do. The penalty for failure to satisfy customer wants is to be put out of business. These schools exemplify that principle; Academy of Our Lady experienced an enrollment decline because of its inability to respond effectively to a market challenge, while Curie Metropolitan High School, despite its shortcomings, had a thriving enrollment and felt no adverse consequences.

Choice is not so different from Chicago school reform as a change strategy. In both cases, school officials can choose to interpret the pressure for change as externally generated and therefore resist it. It is the *perceptions* of those within the school that are critical to its pattern of response and to the eventual role that the pressure will play in bringing school improvement. Formal reforms such as the creation of local school councils or the development of local school improvement plans do not necessarily invoke school improvement, except on paper. In these schools "voice" has been no more a trigger to school improvement than has choice (Cibulka, 1992).

Whenever change is imposed on a school from the outside, whether through a mandate such as the Chicago School Reform Act or through a stress shock such as a market pressure, this is but a precondition for generating school improvement. Given the complexity of schools, it should always come as a surprise when this external signal is interpreted correctly and the organization adapts with a sustained set of planned innovations, followed by success.

Under what circumstances do changes in the "boundary conditions" of an organization, such as the need to redefine its market or to adapt to a new local school council, lead to fundamental school improvement? To answer this question, evaluators of reform can benefit from the literature on planned change in schools. Planned change involves a conscious choice by school authorities to innovate, and the knowledge base on planned change examines how this commitment can lead to effective change processes. Change requires an effective change agent or agents within the school, organizational diagnosis, shared cognitive maps of content and process, trust and rapport building, and institutionalization, to name only some factors. Indeed, Miles (1993) concluded that there are no fewer than twenty-two driving variables that contribute to the development of a new comprehensive map of school change. These variables must include the individual, group, organization, and larger system contexts. In short, in order to grasp why school choice or local school reform work well in some schools and not in others, evaluators must apply the knowledge base on planned change to the individual circumstances in each school and work outward to broader generalizations about why some schools succeed at reform while others do not.

One factor that characterizes the two successful schools examined here, Saint Joseph and Ag School, is the extraordinary leadership of the principals. They were able to use the authority and autonomy at their disposal to define the meaning of the schools' missions and then to select staffs who shared those conceptions. They were involved in curriculum development and concerned themselves with the lives of their pupils, setting an example for other staff. Beyond this factor of leadership, the schools were quite different, of course. Saint Joseph faced significant financial problems and the difficult task of firing staff, which Ag School did not confront.

More attention needs to be paid to these successful cases of planned change if we are to understand how they might be replicated in the education restructuring that is now much discussed. Some analyses of restructuring recognize this complexity (Lieberman, Darling-Hammond, and Zuckerman, 1991; David, 1990). But, overall, the first generation of restructuring literature (for example, Elmore and Associates, 1990; Murphy, 1991) has been preoccupied with clarifying what restructuring actually entails. When evaluators of reform wed their work more directly to the work on planned change, which has been underway for decades, we can look forward to a greater understanding of school reform.

Appendix: Research Methods

This research is an outgrowth of U.S. Department of Education Grant R117E80031, for which the author was a coprincipal investigator. The study involved an initial eighteen-month period of research, followed up to the present at a subset of schools. The total sample included four Catholic high schools and six public high schools of choice in Chicago and Milwaukee. The broad purpose of the study, briefly stated, was to determine under what conditions a good match occurs between student and family wants and needs, on the one hand, and learning opportunities offered by a school, on the other.

A research team of senior faculty and doctoral students collected these data: (1) observation at the school in a variety of locations within and adjacent to the school, over a period of several months; (2) observation of classrooms in four basic subjects, ranging across students' ability levels; (3) interviews with a cross section of senior students and their parents, examination of their transcripts, and interviews with their teachers and counselors; (4) study of school documents and records pertaining to curriculum, grading, discipline, admissions, publicity, and related matters; (5) interviews with school administrative and program staff, community leaders, and central office personnel.

More complete information is available from James G. Cibulka, P. O. Box 413, University of Wisconsin-Milwaukee, Milwaukee, WI 53201.

References

Chubb, J., and Moe, T. *Politics, Markets, and America's Schools.* Washington, D.C.: Brookings Institute, 1990.

Cibulka, J. G. "Local School Reform: The Changing Shape of Educational Politics in Chicago." In K. K. Wong (ed.), *Research in Urban Policy.* Vol. 4. Greenwich, Conn.: JAI Press, 1992.

Coleman, J. S., and Hoffer, T. *Public and Private High Schools: The Impact of Communities.* New York: Basic Books, 1987.

David, J. L. "Restructuring in Progress: Lessons from Pioneering Districts." In R. F. Elmore and Associates (eds.), *Restructuring Schools: The Next Generation of Educational Reform.* San Francisco: Jossey-Bass, 1990.

Elmore, R. F., and Associates. *Restructuring Schools: The Next Generation of Educational Reform.* San Francisco: Jossey-Bass, 1990.

Haertel, E. H., James, T., and Levin, H. M. (eds.). *Comparing Public and Private High Schools*. Vol. 2: *School Achievement*. New York: Falmer Press, 1987.

Lieberman, A., Darling-Hammond, L., and Zuckerman, D. *Early Lessons in Restructuring Schools*. New York: National Center for Restructuring Education, Schools, and Teaching, Teachers College, Columbia University, 1991.

Miles, M. B. "40 Years of Change in Schools: Some Personal Reflections." *Educational Administration Quarterly*, 1993, *30* (2), 323–340.

Moore, D., and Davenport, S. "School Choice: The New Improved Sorting Machine." In W. L. Boyd and H. J. Walberg (eds.), *Choice in Education: Potential and Problems*. Berkeley, Calif.: McCutchan, 1990.

Murphy, J. *Restructuring Schools: Capturing and Assessing the Phenomena*. New York: Teachers College Press, 1991.

Wong, K. K. "Choice in Public Schools: Their Institutional Functions and Distributive Consequences." In K. K. Wong (ed.), *Research in Urban Policy*. Vol. 4. Greenwich, Conn.: JAI Press, 1992.

JAMES G. CIBULKA *is professor of administrative leadership and a faculty member in the doctoral program in urban education at the University of Wisconsin, Milwaukee.*

This chapter examines changes in how and what children are taught in the Chicago public schools since reform legislation was enacted. The authors examine the Coalition of Essential Schools, the Paideia Program, the Algebra Project, and the Home and Hospital programs.

School Reform and the Curriculum

Melanie F. Sikorski, Trudy Wallace,
Winifred E. Stariha, Vivian E. Rankin

The Chicago School Reform Act of 1988 transferred the power to make important school decisions from central office bureaucrats to local schools. The rationale for the act was that the system was too large and the problems too complex for one set of policies, curricula, or classroom practices to work systemwide. The law established that the most democratic way to reverse the dismal academic performance of the city's schools was to shift almost all of the authority to run local schools to those who have a stake in the schools' performance—presumably, the communities, parents, and teachers and administrators.

Through local school councils (LSCs) and Professional Personnel Advisory Committees (PPACs), members of the communities and teachers decide not only on changes in governance and personnel but also on such issues as dress and discipline codes, after-school programs to address local problems, and changes in curricula and classroom practices. The last mentioned is perhaps the most important. Without improvements in the curricula and instruction, it seems doubtful that student academic performance can be greatly improved. Poor academic performance was perhaps the most compelling reason for the law in the first place.

This chapter focuses on changes in how and what students are taught in the Chicago public schools. We examine four different programs that were created or whose implementation was accelerated in response to the reform effort. These include the Coalition of Essential Schools (CES), the Paideia Program, the Algebra Project, and the Home and Hospital programs that serve students who are unable to attend school. Each program is described and its evaluation evidence summarized.

NEW DIRECTIONS FOR PROGRAM EVALUATION, no. 59, Fall 1993 © Jossey-Bass Publishers

Coalition of Essential Schools

Since the early 1980s, Theodore Sizer, former dean of the Harvard Graduate School of Education and headmaster of Phillips Exeter Academy, has been helping to restructure American secondary schools through CES. The program is based at Brown University and currently has approximately 140 member schools nationwide, of which 11 are part of the Chicago Public School System. With training from a network of CES facilitators and financial support from foundation and corporation grants, member schools seek to improve academic performance through a series of faculty inservices, new course development, and curriculum modifications.

CES is built around nine beliefs about education called the Common Principles. Clearly, the philosophical underpinnings are Deweyan. The program is student-centered, and learning is intended to be experiential, relevant, and personalized. The reflective learner actively participates in this process and demonstrates mastery in a variety of ways. The teacher is a coach or facilitator as opposed to a dispenser of knowledge.

Teachers in Essential Schools borrow strategies commonly found in cooperative learning environments and collaborative classrooms, and they borrow from effective schools' practices. Students tackle problems or issues in depth, engaging their minds in complex and comprehensive thinking. They investigate serious subject matter and problems, not only in the schools but also in community centers, public libraries, community colleges, and churches. They employ such techniques as oral histories, focus groups, and videotaping to acquire competencies and master knowledge.

In the Essential School classroom, teachers and students become partners in the learning process. As generalists, the teachers provide ways to learn rather than focus on specific content areas. Teachers are generalists first and subject area specialists second. Teachers and students become stakeholders in the learning process by setting goals, determining outcomes, defining activities and strategies, and, finally, defining how competencies and mastery will be demonstrated.

Every student can and is expected to learn. Each is expected to master a limited number of essential skills and areas of knowledge. If students enter secondary schools without appropriate skills, they are provided with intensive remediation to help them quickly meet standards. They work in an atmosphere of "unanxious expectations." Students can expect to be treated fairly and decently.

One basic tenet of Essential Schools is the "less is more" concept. A paring down of the electives of the "shopping mall" curriculum to a core set of essential skills is the first step in transforming the secondary school. The intent is to turn from survey courses to in-depth examinations of a core curriculum. Typically, courses are taught in tandem. For example, an English teacher may collaborate with a humanities or social sciences teacher to offer an in-depth investigation of the literature of the American Civil War or, perhaps, Tudor England. Two physics teachers may build on each other's strengths with one supervising all laboratory work and the other presenting all lectures.

Students in Essential Schools are evaluated through performance assessments. In addition to paper-and-pencil tests, students demonstrate mastery through exhibitions. These include best-sample portfolios, art projects and photography, video and tape recordings, demonstrations, oral defenses, and summary résumés of community involvement and internships.

To accomplish the goals of Essential Schools, teacher-pupil ratios should not exceed 1:80. In addition, administrators should establish substantial common planning periods for coteachers. This may result in a reduction or realignment of present course offerings in the schools.

At present, there are eleven Chicago public high schools in CES. The membership and composition of the schools reflect citywide distribution. Each of the schools was given a three-year, $95,000 implementation grant. To have become part of CES, 75 percent of each school's faculty had to have voted affirmatively. Representative faculty members participated in conferences and staff development workshops and seminars in and out of state. CES provided each school with a facilitator.

To evaluate a program's effectiveness, we examined achievement, graduation, attendance, and dropout rates and American College Test (ACT) scores for all eleven schools from the time they became CES members. In addition, we interviewed personnel from several of the schools. All data were collected from the annual school report cards (required by Illinois law) for three years prior and subsequent to membership. Achievement data included the reading comprehension and mathematics components of the Test of Achievement and Proficiency (TAP) and the Illinois Goal Assessment Program.

Students in all eleven CES schools declined in reading achievement and in ten out of eleven schools declined in mathematics from 1988–89 to 1991–92, as measured by the TAP. The percentage of students scoring at or above national norms declined in eleventh grade an average of 28 percent in reading. Only 18 percent of eleventh graders in reading and 17 percent in mathematics scored at or above national norms. Achievement data on the Illinois Goal Assessment Program, although better, still presented a bleak picture. Only four of the eleven schools improved in reading achievement. In 1991–92, 25 percent of students scored in the top two quartiles.

During the period of investigation, one school's graduation rate increased substantially, two remained the same, and the remaining eight decreased substantially. The range of decline in graduation rates was from 3 to 64 percent. Attendance rates declined in all schools. The average rate of decline was 8 percent. In nine of the eleven schools, the dropout rate increased an average of 39 percent. Two schools reported a decreased dropout rate.

There was one area in which students did improve. Average composite ACT scores increased at all schools. These scores were recorded by students who had completed college preparatory coursework. However, the students who completed the necessary coursework for college entrance represented less than 2 percent of the students in the eleven CES high schools. In addition, the higher dropout rates meant that the students who remained were a more select, less representative group.

These data indicate the Essential Schools implementation has not benefited indicators of quality education in Chicago. There are a number of reasons for this outcome. One is poor or scattered implementation. All of the schools exceeded the 1:80 faculty-student ratio. At one school, the administration seemed more interested in grant funding than in the CES philosophy. Another reason is the environment created by the reform movement. In the shift of control from central office to local school, the emphasis in the local schools has been on governance issues rather than academic progress. If Essential Schools are to be successful in Chicago, more substantial changes are needed.

Paideia Program

The Paideia Program derives its inspiration from Mortimer Adler's (1982) *Paideia Proposal: An Educational Manifesto*. The model emphasizes high academic achievement expectations and features increased use of original literary sources, such as the works of Aesop, Gwendolyn Brooks, Cervantes, Martin Luther King, Jr., Blake, and Plato. Seminar readings are selected on the basis of their challenge to the reader and are not limited to "great books." Paideia features three modes of teaching: didactic (lecturing), coaching (supervised practice), and Socratic (seminars devoted to questioning to develop thinking and self-expression). The chief purpose of the Socratic seminar is to develop students' literacy—their ability to think critically and communicate ideas—by enlarging their understanding of books.

In Chicago, the Paideia Program at each school is coordinated by a teacher. The program has grown from four to over twenty-five elementary and high schools. The schools represent socioeconomic, ethnic, and achievement diversity. More than five thousand students in grades K–12 are now in the Paideia Program. A teacher reeducation component in the liberal arts and sciences focuses on the development of Socratic seminar techniques. Instructional formats include a two-week summer institute at Saint John's College in Santa Fe, New Mexico, the Paideia Graduate Institute at the University of Illinois at Urbana-Champaign, the University of Illinois at Chicago, and the Paideia Institute of Hyde Park; and after-school seminars and weekend retreats conducted by staff from Saint John's College, the University of Chicago, Loyola University, and the Adler Institute for Philosophical Research.

Paideia offers a departure from the traditional approach to education. In this environment, teachers and students read, write, talk, and think together. Using instructional strategies consistent with the Socratic method, teachers establish and follow a line of inquiry, elicit responses from participants, ask probing initial questions, employ follow-up questions that encourage exploration of multiple dimensions of the texts, allow adequate student response time, and repeat and rephrase questions when necessary.

Mortimer Adler described the Socratic method as the art of questioning. Socratic seminar techniques, developed through training and experience, include the following: playing the devil's advocate, beginning the seminar with a maximum of two questions, posing questions that have no right or wrong answers, asking thought-provoking questions, asking students to prepare opening questions, focusing on a controversial aspect of the text, looking for inconsistencies in the text, and discussing the text selection with a colleague.

Reticent students pose a unique challenge. Seminar leaders use a repertoire of methods to draw them into the discussion, such as posing direct questions to class members, talking to quieter students prior to the seminar, having students prepare written questions, asking quiet students to read aloud from the text, having students draw from personal experience to develop the discussion, having students summarize an argument, pairing the reluctant student with a more outgoing participant, and having the reticent student report the results of the discussion.

Students who dominate discussion represent a threat to the intent of a seminar to involve each member of the group. The techniques that teachers use to control dominant members include asking them to wait until three other seminar participants speak, count to five before commenting, sit outside the group and take notes, listen to the ideas of others, limit their response times, and behave courteously when others speak.

The amount of class time allocated to the Paideia Program strands is nine hour per week for didactic instruction, two hours per week for a Socratic seminar, and one hour per week for coaching, on average. Coaching consists of individual tutoring to develop writing skills, practice in specific skills, follow-up seminar activities, and remediation exercises.

Wallace (1990) conducted an extensive evaluation of Paideia for the Chicago Board of Education. She concluded that the program had many positive effects, including higher attendance rates, enhanced student achievement and attitudes, and decreased student failures. In addition, students in the Paideia Program appeared to express and support their ideas significantly better than students in the comparison groups. Fewer Paideia students failed subjects and missed school than did students citywide. Participating teachers reported that 3.6 percent of Paideia elementary students failed English, mathematics, or science compared with 4.3 percent of elementary students citywide who were not promoted.

Using TAP results as an index of academic progress, we found that 33 to 66 percent of non-Paideia students in Paideia high schools scored in the bottom quartile in reading comprehension, mathematical problem solving, and science. On average, only 11 percent of Paideia high school students failed these subjects.

Attendance data indicated that Paideia students attended high school more regularly than did non-Paideia students. At two Paideia Program high schools, average daily attendance for Paideia students was 84 percent and 91 percent, compared to 78 percent and 85 percent for non-Paideia students. It is difficult to know to what extent these differences are attributable to student selection rather than to program effects.

To determine whether or not the Paideia Program fosters growth in critical thinking skills and overall literacy, staff of the Department of Research, Evaluation, and Planning of the Chicago public schools administered writing assessment items from the 1981 National Assessment of Educational Progress to 196 (79 Paideia and 117 comparison) students. Each writing sample was scored by raters on the student's ability to identify a characteristic or mood in a poem prompt and substantiate it with contextual, stylistic, or subjective evidence from the poem. The scorers' interrater agreement was .91. The results of the writing assessment indicated a substantial advantage for the Paideia students, who expressed and supported their ideas significantly better than did students in the comparison groups.

In 1991, school improvement plans collected and reviewed by staff from the Department of Research, Evaluation, and Planning indicated that sixty-nine schools planned to use the Paideia program or Socratic seminars as strategies to improve student achievement in reading, writing, mathematics, and higher-order thinking; to meet staff development goals; to provide a common learning experience; and to serve students with special needs. In 1992, ninety-one school improvement plans selected Paideia as a strategy to meet these reform goals. As part of school reform, school improvement plans, which outline strategies to be used to attain reform goals, must be developed annually and implemented by all Chicago public schools.

Surveys developed by staff from the Department of Research, Evaluation, and Planning were sent to a sample of six Paideia schools to assess the perceptions of program teachers, students, and parents. Survey responses from 134 second- through twelfth-grade Paideia students were analyzed. Students reported participating in thirty-five Socratic seminars, generally in English or language arts class, during the school year—on average, about once a week. Most students described the seminars as positive learning experiences: 63 percent reported that they liked being in a seminar discussion better than listening to a teacher's lecture, 57 percent said that the seminar readings were interesting, 67 percent were able to participate in the class discussions as often as they wished, but 32 percent said that there were too many people in the seminar groups (a previous evaluation of Paideia recommended a maximum of 20 students per seminar).

Program outcomes included increases in students' ability to organize thoughts more quickly (68 percent), talk about a subject (67 percent), write better stories, essays, and letters (66 percent), and organize thoughts better (65 percent). Affective program outcomes were increases in students' ability to understand themselves (75 percent), understand other people (74 percent), respect their teachers (72 percent), and work with others (69 percent).

Survey responses from nineteen Paideia high school teachers indicated that sixteen of them conducted one seminar a week, and seventeen gave one writing assignment a week, on average. In general, teachers' ratings were higher than those of their students, but only 60 percent of teachers said that they preferred conducting a Socratic seminar over giving a lecture (compared to 63 percent of students who preferred a seminar over a lecture). Teachers said that students participated in discussions as often as they wanted (79 percent), thought the seminar readings were interesting (71 percent), and showed interest in the seminar discussion (68 percent); 29 percent of teachers said that seminar groups were too large.

Teachers reported that the program increased students' ability to discuss a topic (90 percent), organize thoughts (82 percent), work with others (74 percent), like school better (70 percent), enjoy reading (69 percent), and respect teachers (68 percent). Although 82 percent of teachers reported that sufficient faculty seminars and in-services were provided to implement the Paideia Program, 58 percent said that additional staff training is needed to support more effective implementation of Paideia.

Within the sample of 120 parents of kindergarten through twelfth-grade students in the program, 70 percent said that the schools kept them well informed about Paideia, and 65 percent described their children's Paideia programs as well planned. Parents reported that the programs increased their children's ability to read (76 percent), think better (72 percent), and speak better (72 percent) and increased their children's excitement for school (68 percent) and self-esteem (60 percent); 80 percent of parents said that they wanted their children to remain in the Paideia Program.

Is Paideia a viable program for education reform? Evaluation results are important because they demonstrate that urban students can benefit educationally when literacy is taught effectively. The Paideia Program had positive effects on students' writing and reasoning ability. The seminar proved to be a potent activity where students could express their ideas, reason and think, and actively argue and substantiate their differences of opinion with facts and related opinion. Program teachers, students, and their parents reported increases in students' self-esteem, respect for their teachers, and liking for school. The evaluation results suggest that Paideia is a successful strategy for attaining reform goals such as development of students' writing and thinking skills, staff development, and establishment of a common learning experience. Further evaluation of Paideia is needed to assess its effectiveness in achieving other important education reform goals.

Algebra Project

The Algebra Project is currently implemented in nineteen elementary schools in Chicago and is known as the Chicago Algebra Project (CAP). The curriculum uses everyday experiences to help students in grades six to eight understand algebraic concepts. The project's philosophy is that all students should be exposed to algebra regardless of prior achievement. The project involves the home, community, and school in the development of activities that support student achievement and offers a model of intellectual development that is based on motivation rather than ability.

Much of the developmental work on the Algebra Project was done by Robert P. Moses, a community activist and mathematics teacher in New York and Africa (see Moses, Kamii, Swap, and Howard, 1989). He challenged some of the implicit assumptions of school systems concerning mathematics achievement and minority students. He believes that motivation is far more important for achievement than is ability. To foster this motivation to achieve, he draws analogies to community efforts in the civil rights movement of the 1960s.

The Algebra Project uses a five-step teaching and learning process that takes students from a physical event to its symbolic representation: (1) physical event, (2) picture or model of the event, (3) intuitive (idiomatic) language description of the event, (4) description of the event in regimented English, and (5) symbolic representation of the event. The purpose of the five steps is to ground students in concrete examples of abstract concepts. An often-cited example of the project is a ride on the subway line. This context serves as a basis for questions. In which station do we start? End? How many stops in between? When they return, students are asked to write about, draw a picture of, or construct a three-dimensional model of their trip. They can also make graphs or other displays. This pictorial depiction helps to fix the concepts in the students' minds. The subway ride serves as the basis for developing an understanding of the abstract concepts of the number line and the use of integers. This teaching method suggests that a child's learning should be a constructive social activity. The first steps are intended to facilitate symbolic representation, which is achieved through the last of the five steps. This entire process presumably helps students recognize the origin and the development of symbols.

CAP is founded on community involvement and is part of the school reform movement in Chicago. This project acknowledges the mistaken assumptions that mathematics demands an inherent ability and that people of color are unable to learn mathematics. One of the project's goals is to increase the proportion and total number of minority students entering the college preparatory sequence in mathematics and science at high school entrance.

Implementation of CAP began with a seven-day training program for forty-five instructors in January 1991. Members of community-based organizations, teachers, principals, and LSC members were trained. During the pilot year, the project gave instruction to more than eight hundred students in twenty-nine sixth-grade classrooms.

Phase 1 provided training for sixth-grade teachers in six schools. Phase 2 brought five additional schools to the project and provided training for seventh- and eighth-grade teachers from the pilot schools. In September 1992, phase 3 began in eight schools.

In keeping with school reform, the CAP schools were asked to get their LSCs to approve and faculty to commit to the project's implementation in the sixth, seventh, and eighth grades over three years. In sixth grade, students are taught the CAP curriculum for an equivalent of a semester's instruction during the school year. In grades seven and eight, students have two years to finish a standard Algebra I textbook along with additional modules developed by Robert Moses. In addition to the original training of the instructors, monthly follow-up training sessions are provided to the participants, involving a half-day on-site visit to each school. CAP is increasing the local training capacity by involving assistant trainers who help teachers in the effective implementation of the curriculum.

The Iowa Test of Basic Skills (ITBS) mathematics scores of the sixth-grade students involved in CAP phases 1 and 2 were reviewed to determine whether CAP had an impact on the scores. We compared the CAP classes and a cohort of sixth-grade mathematics students from the previous year who did not have CAP instruction. Percentages from the individual grades are reported in quartiles, and grade-level scores are reported at the school, subdistrict, and district levels.

The cohort group were the sixth-graders in the schools reported in phase 1 who took the ITBS mathematics subtest in 1990. When the 1991 ITBS mathematics test was given, the CAP students had been receiving instruction since January 1991. In phase 2, the cohort group included students taking the ITBS in 1991, while the 1992 students had the benefit of the CAP instruction. On the school level, looking at the top and bottom quartiles, 1991 results show that among the phase 1 CAP schools three of the six schools had a lower percentage of students in the top quartile and four of the six had a higher percentage of students in the bottom quartile than those in the previous year who were not in the project. Percentages also indicated that the students in the top quartile in six of the CAP schools were slightly lower that those who did not receive instruction. The CAP schools had a higher percentage of students scoring in the bottom quartile than did the sixth-grade cohorts in non-CAP schools. The district or citywide results exhibited a very slight decrease in the percentages of students scoring in the top quartile of CAP schools and an increase in the percentages of those students scoring in the bottom quartile.

School-level scores in phase 2 of CAP revealed that more students scored in the top quartile in three CAP schools and lower in two CAP schools. More students scored in the bottom quartile in four of the five CAP schools. The top-quartile percentages remained the same in two schools in both the cohort and CAP groups; two of the CAP schools were lower than non-CAP schools, and one CAP school was 1 percent higher. All of the CAP schools had a higher percentage in the bottom quartile than did non-CAP schools. At the district level, the top-quartile percentages were the same in both 1991 and 1992. The number of students scoring in the bottom quartile increased by 1 percent in CAP schools. Phase 3 schools entered CAP in September 1992 and scores are currently not available.

The results do not indicate a significant positive CAP impact on ITBS mathematics scores. However, comparison of the ITBS total mathematics scores of CAP sixth graders and a cohort group is but one method of looking at the influence of this project, which is still being developed and presented in the CAP schools. A more formal and comprehensive evaluation of the entire project is still in the planning stage. This evaluation will assess CAP's effect on achievement, on students' mathematics and science-related aspirations, and on the teaching of mathematics, as well as the project's role in developing communities that seek to solve the problem of mathematics illiteracy.

There are, of course impediments to implementation of curriculum innovations in urban schools. Schools may be willing to implement the innovations but still want to complete their conventional curricula. Many teachers believe that students must master previously required material. Concern about performance on standardized tests influences the preparation of students using traditional methods and materials.

Mathematics instructors, moreover, are hesitant to change their approach. In CAP, they must move from a lecture method to discussion and develop a cooperative learning environment for an experientially based approach. They must also seek consensus in support of their efforts in the school, community, and central office. This may be too much to ask in an extraordinary period of reform. Perhaps more time will yield better circumstances, encouragement, implementation—results.

Home and Hospital Programs

The Home and Hospital programs are designed to provide continuing education services to students whose medical conditions prohibit school attendance. Until 1990, when it was restructured, the programs were managed by central office personnel, with satellite offices in schools for the physically handicapped. A cadre of seventy-seven teachers was budgeted for students who were confined to their homes or to hospitals. In keeping with the spirit of local control of the schools, the Home and Hospital programs were restructured under the reform effort. Sixty-four teaching positions were eliminated. Local schools were responsible for providing home teaching services using classroom teachers working after school. In this section, we describe both delivery models and compare their effectiveness and costs.

Prior to 1990, the Home and Hospital programs operated under a delivery model that had been in place since the 1950s. To access homebound services, the student's physician completed a medical referral form, which was then processed by central office personnel. It was then sent to the Bureau of Medical and Health Services for review. Upon approval of a board of education medical consultant, one of the cadre of teachers was assigned to the student. The teacher would contact the school for academic information and arrange with the parent for home visits.

Often, it would take two weeks to process the papers. If the teachers had full caseloads, it would sometimes take a month before students received services. It was also difficult to provide appropriately certified teachers, especially for bilingual or high school students taking advanced coursework in science, mathematics, or foreign languages.

With changes in medical practices, the number of children hospitalized for long periods of time has decreased dramatically, but the number of children confined to their home has increased. Children in hospitals were typically grouped into homogeneous units and taught by one or two teachers stationed permanently at each hospital. Usually, small classrooms and curriculum libraries were maintained to service the needs of the students. Once the number of hospitalized students declined, it was no longer cost-effective to permanently assign teachers to hospitals.

In a homebound environment, where teachers must travel to see all students, one and one-half hours were allocated daily for travel. Further, each teacher had to travel individually to the student's home, and travel could often take up one or more hours a day depending on location, season, and other factors.

Despite several attempts to maximize efficiency, the basic centralized service delivery was cumbersome and inefficient. Even with the activities of seventy-seven teachers, many students went unserved, and budgetary constraints prohibited the hiring of additional teachers. The situation had bogged down to the point that by 1990, two complaints were filed with the U.S. Office of Civil Rights, based on Section 504 of the Rehabilitation Act. (Under this provision, an individual is handicapped if he or she has a physical or mental impairment that substantially limits one of more major life activities, has a record of an impairment, or is regarded as having a disability.)

To resolve the complaints, the Chicago public schools agreed to make necessary changes to comply with the law. The school system could have maintained the education services delivery model and allocated more resources to it but opted instead for a model based on service delivery from local schools. Of the seventy-seven teachers at the central office, sixty-two were reassigned to other positions and the remaining fifteen were used to provide services in hospitals.

The new model transferred responsibility for educating homebound students to the local schools. Once appropriate medical documents were filed, principals appointed teachers to provide service to the students in their homes before or after school hours. The classroom teacher was encouraged to serve as the home teacher and received additional compensation. In addition, a citywide pool of teachers was developed for those cases in which no local teacher was willing to serve as a home teacher. This resolved the difficulty in identifying certified teachers qualified in technical subjects, foreign languages, and laboratory sciences. In the new delivery model, hospital services remained essentially the same.

Use of the student's own teacher solved many problems of coordinating activities and reduced transition concerns. The classroom teacher, with knowledge of the curriculum, could continue with instruction with little or no loss of continuity. Teachers became increasingly sensitive to the specific learning and interpersonal styles of their homebound students. Their improved understanding of diverse cultural, racial, and linguistic backgrounds reaped benefits for in-school students as well.

The per-pupil per-day cost using the delivery model prior to reform was approximately $68, with an average annual salary of $40,000 and 25 percent in benefits and miscellaneous expenses. With the reform delivery model, the per-pupil per-day cost is only $36—almost a 50 percent reduction. This estimate is probably conservative as not all teachers under the previous model were utilized 100 percent of the time.

Conclusion

Dozens of programs in multiple Chicago public schools might have been studied to gain a sense of how reform has affected them. The facts about the four programs reviewed here, however, may represent what a much more comprehensive evaluation is likely to show. Under school reform, school staff are capable of choosing and implementing well-known, highly regarded curriculum programs; Essential Schools and Paideia are notable examples. Despite high regard in the profession, these programs have been subject to little rigorous evaluation in the nation. Nor have the evaluations in Chicago reported in this chapter been as comprehensive and systematic as one would wish.

It is nonetheless encouraging that parents and teachers appear to think well of the programs. At the same time, it is discouraging that schools employing the programs did no better or, in several cases, worse on objective measures of school achievement, especially in view of the centrality of achievement gains in the reform plan.

It is similarly discouraging to have little learning gains to show for CAP and CES. Perhaps, though, the fact that a "foreign program," CAP, is in place and running is accomplishment enough given the preoccupation of LSCs and other parties with governance and budgetary issues rather than learning. Similarly, the administrative transformation of the Home and Hospital programs to fit the restructuring must count for something. If patient, policymakers may find that such changes in means eventually result in better outcomes.

References

Adler, M. J. *The Paideia Proposal: An Educational Manifesto.* New York: Macmillan, 1982.

Moses, R. P., Kamii, M., Swap, S., and Howard, J. "The Algebra Project: Organizing in the Spirit of Ella." *Harvard Educational Review*, 1989, 59 (4).

Wallace, T. *Evaluation of the 1987–88 Paideia Program.* Chicago: Chicago Board of Education, 1990.

MELANIE F. SIKORSKI *teaches in the Chicago public schools (CPSs). She also works in the CPS Department of Research, Evaluation, and Planning.*

TRUDY WALLACE *is coordinator of evaluation in the CPS Department of Research, Evaluation, and Planning.*

WINIFRED E. STARIHA *is an administrator in the CPS Department of Special Education and Pupil Support Services.*

VIVIAN E. RANKIN *is coordinator of the CPS Home and Hospital programs.*

School reform has deeply affected the education and business communities in Chicago. In this chapter, three prominent Chicagoans assess reform and its impact.

Three Perspectives on School Reform

Asish Sen, Jacqueline B. Vaughn, Thomas Flanagan

Chicago School Reform: A Highly Personal Assessment

Asish Sen

After the passage of the Chicago School Reform Act by the Illinois legislature in December 1988, Chicago embarked on what has been hailed as one the most ambitious experiments in American education. The reform act was a response to years of poor student achievement. Perhaps because much of the concern over performance centered on dropout rates, and perhaps also because of the grass-roots tradition in Chicago, reform in Chicago was based on the theory that democratic control at the school site level would lead to better schools. In this way at least, school reform in Chicago was unique.

However, the reform act included several elements, some of which are clearly there to appease various interests. While I cannot examine all of these elements, I must mention one that has had significant impact on the schools. This is the part of the act that requires state Chapter I funds, which are allotted to school districts on the basis of numbers of low income and underperforming students, to be distributed (gradually, over a five-year period) to schools within the district according to the same criterion. Moreover, Chapter I funds allocated to schools cannot be used for purposes similar to those of general school funds; rather, they must be used for supplementary purposes, though totally at the discretion of the school. This element in the act, which requires reallocation of $300 million by the 1993–94 school year, has been largely responsible for increasing the number of teachers in the public schools and speeding up the arrival of computer education in the schools.

Although opinions differ, I believe that implementation of the reform act, which was largely left up to the Chicago Board of Education and the general superintendent, was carried out about as well as one could expect. Local School Councils (LSCs) have been in place for three years. While some LSCs have had difficulty getting a quorum at many of their meetings, on the whole they have been effective. They have selected principals, as they were required to do. School improvement plans have been drawn up, district councils have been elected, and board of education members have been appointed through a complex process. In this context, it must be pointed out that while restructuring costs money, no funds were made available for implementation of reform.

An assessment of the success of reform depends on which effects one chooses to examine. The number of teachers in schools has increased, and some schools have been able to get better equipment. There is clearly greater community involvement. There is a higher level of enthusiasm throughout the system and a new spirit of openness in the way in which the board of education and its senior staff conduct business.

On the other hand, democratic participation in school governance has been less than overwhelming. Given that most of those voting in LSC elections were eligible to vote in several schools and probably did, I estimate that less than 5 percent of eligible voters cast ballots.

There has also been little perceptible improvement in student performance on tests. Some may argue that we need to give reform more time. However, I do not believe that reform will substantially affect student achievement. Although, two years ago, I was very enthusiastic about the potential of reform to positively affect student performance, hindsight suggests that reform had little chance of achieving this end. Concerned mainly with governance of the school system, it is too far removed from the individual student to have much direct effect. If more learning is to occur, a child needs to spend more time at it and also use this time more intensively. Reform seems to have had little effect either on the amount time a student spends studying or in the way this time is spent.

Thus, it seems quite clear to me that if student achievement is to improve, something more has to occur—perhaps Reform II. Is the governance machinery set up by reform better able than the prereform structure to design and implement Reform II? I do not know the answer to this question, but I certainly hope that it is yes.

Transforming Our Schools: The Move from Reform to Restructuring

Jacqueline B. Vaughn
The focus of school reform in Chicago must shift from concerns of school site governance and school site management to the radical transformation of our schools into effective places of learning. The Chicago Teachers

Union believes that we must make this move from reform to restructuring to enable students to better prepare for their futures. The steps that have been taken thus far to reform our city's schools are only tentative, and much is left to be done. While the reform mandates provide the opportunity for school staff to change their instructional programs, the new programs can only be judged successful or failing ventures when measured against other school programs. These same mandates also provide an opportunity for schools to establish on-site communities, thus far composed of people who share educational values and vision. The school-based management mandate has not been in operation long enough to yield long-term effective change, reflecting measurable dramatic impact on teaching and learning.

Since the traditional factory model of teaching and learning does not prepare today's youth for working in an information and technological age, teaching and learning focused on the highest of academic standards must be the core concern of our schools.

Extensive research has demonstrated that in order to actively engage students in the learning process, that process must relate to the learner's world. Since learning is a social process, learners do best when they can relate the process to activities with which they are familiar. Research also has shown that students learn at different rates and at different times. We know that students should be engaged in complex tasks in order to challenge and stimulate interests. We also know that a uniform approach to learning and a single method of instruction are characteristic of the factory model of learning.

Such research-based theories about learning are incompatible with the way in which schools are now structured. A new vision of learning requires a new vision and blueprint of the teaching-learning process. Schools must be restructured so that decisions promote active, engaged, individual learning and emphasize depth of understanding and higher levels of thinking. Restructuring must involve the educators responsible for implementing the restructured process.

In a restructured school, the students will be engaged in the process of learning rather than passively receiving information. The teacher will serve as facilitator of knowledge. There will be a focus on individual learning rates. This will require different ways of grouping students and flexible scheduling that can accommodate learning at different rates of speed. Such nontraditional approaches as multiage grouping, staff teams working with the same students over three to five years, and nongraded interdisciplinary classrooms should be developed and implemented.

We must also realign the connections between schools and the real world since we live in an age of rapidly changing technology that must be incorporated into the curriculum along with other out-of-school experiences. In this new blueprint for learning, all of our assumptions concerning education must be revised.

New organizational reforms require new roles for those involved. The role of teacher will shift from disseminator of information to facilitator of knowledge, from expert to coach, from instructional worker to instructional leader. The role of the student changes from the recipient of information to knowledge worker, from passive receptor to active learner. The principal's role changes from supervisor to collegial leader who enables and supports teams of teachers and classroom assistants in roles that more effectively serve students. Principals should continue to manage the resources needed to get the job done. The role for the classroom assistant will also change from helper to team member as he or she assumes more complex and sophisticated tasks. Such collaboration and organizational structure may resemble a hospital where diverse health care professionals work together with the common goal of improving the health of the patient.

Since teachers are the key component in Chicago's instructional process, the quality, commitment, and morale of our teaching force are absolute priorities. Educational policymakers who fail to recognize these priorities lack the ability to effectively deal with strategic planning for our city's schools. We need a three-faceted commitment over the next decade so that educational and support staff involved in this system will enter the twenty-first century with an established vision and plan for instituting quality education. This commitment will require the creation of different and better ways of recruiting, selecting, preparing, and training people who wish to teach. It will also require investment of capital and human resources in the further professional development of our existing teaching force, in order to change the current notion of schooling, teaching, and learning. The need to involve teachers directly in the restructuring of instructional programs is based on research on the development of a new learning process. G. Alfred Hess, Jr., in his book *School Restructuring, Chicago Style,* commented on the future of reform in this city: "If teachers do not become involved in the change process at the local school level, it is unlikely that any significant differences will be experienced by students."

We must develop teachers who can provide leadership for the changes in the teaching and learning process needed to prepare students to meet evolving national standards. The Chicago School Reform Act has opened the door for teachers and other school employees to take a more active role in restructuring the education process. Edward B. Fiske, in his book *Smart School, Smart Kids,* stated that "this massive exercise in educational democracy and decentralization has raised the hopes of thousands of parents and teachers that they can find workable solutions to their problems."

The Chicago Teachers Union believes that schools and the teaching-learning process must be radically altered within the next decade. Change from within is necessary if public schools are to continue to play an essential role in the development of a well-educated and active citizenry, which is so vital to our society. The union is committed to guiding and training teachers and educational support staff in implementing significant changes required in our classrooms.

In order for our city's schools to move boldly toward this transformation, there are several major issues that must be addressed.

- Professionalizing teaching to meet the demands of this new paradigm
- Restructuring the teaching-learning process
- Establishing a fair and equitable financial base to support our schools
- Strengthening the relationship between home and school, parent and teacher
- Creating incentives for change: rewards for success and innovations and well-defined sanctions for failure
- Redefining the role of administrator

The Chicago Teachers Union believes that these issues must be addressed through aggressive initiatives that reflect the values of professionalism and the enhancement of the teaching-learning process. Toward this end, the union has developed programs designed to provide leadership in confronting these issues directly through careful planning and implementation. The following are examples of these initiatives.

The Chicago Teachers Union Quest Center operates under a $1 million support fund from the MacArthur Foundation to act as a catalyst in transforming our public schools. The center acts as a clearinghouse for information, models, and staff development in school restructuring ideas. It will also target ten to fifteen schools each year for support and incentive awards for radical changes that will result in higher achievement for students.

Teachers for Chicago is a collaborative effort with the Golden Apple Foundation, the Chicago Board of Education, and the Chicago Area Council of Deans of Education to establish a two-year internship program for training and mentoring new teachers. The program will involve two hundred teachers each year. It is funded through a grant from Chicago Community Trust.

The Urban Teacher Selection Program is an innovative research-driven model for training teachers and principals to interview and select prospective teachers for their schools. Presently, there are ten school-level professionals who offer training in this interview process to local school staff.

In addition, the Chicago Teachers Union offers a wide variety of staff development opportunities. These include the Educational Research and Development Program, which provides teachers with the latest research on classroom teaching issues; the Critical Thinking Project, which emphasizes the infusion of higher-level thinking skills into the regular curriculum; and the New Directions in Teacher Decision-Making Program, which assists local teacher committees in local site governance skills and instructional goal setting.

It is essential that teachers, administrators, and concerned citizens engage in serious discussion and debate on the education issues that confront us. The union supports systematic and systemic change. Although substantial discourse has already taken place regarding some of the new initiatives, it is important that we continue the dialogue and utilize information, experience, and research in guiding these positive changes and innovations.

Chicago School Reform: A View from Business

Thomas Flanagan

Every year *Fortune* magazine assesses the business climate in cities around the country, and one of the major criteria the editors use is a sufficiently large enough and properly educated work force. In a May 15, 1989, editorial, the *Chicago Tribune* declared that "Chicago's public school system is failing its children and jeopardizing the city's future." Comparisons of test scores in Chicago with the major markets around the country yielded disastrous results. Chicago's students are last among U.S. cities. In fact, in November 1987, Secretary of Education William Bennett said, "I'm not sure there's a system as bad as the Chicago system. . . . If there's one that's worse, I don't know where it is."

Many suggestions have been offered for improving the performance of the schools, including decentralization, break up of the Chicago Board of Education into smaller units, more training for teachers, and reduction of class size. But these seem like rearrangements of the deck chairs on the *Titanic*. It is time to fix the problem and empower those who can change the system.

One of the basic tenets of American business is that if a goal is important, then measurement of progress toward achieving it is essential. In business, managers and individual contributors have clearly defined roles and specified jobs. If the job is not done, the individual is replaced. If the job still remains unfinished, the manager is replaced. In the Chicago public schools, when the central office bureaucrats ran the schools, students failed, but no one was held responsible. Under school reform, students are still failing and yet still no one is held responsible. Chicago ranks last in educational achievement and yet teachers and principals get pay raises.

It is time to make teachers in Chicago public schools accountable. In fact, all school personnel must be held responsible for doing their jobs if we are to improve the education of our children. Teachers should teach effectively, closely monitor student progress, reteach where necessary, and assign homework. They should also identify children who may need more help and should alert parents and school administrators to take necessary steps to ensure success. If they do not, they should be counseled.

Principals should monitor teacher behavior closely. There is no need to wait for end-of-the-year statistics to know that achievement and attendance are down. Monitoring should be done monthly, and if trends are declining, necessary action should be taken. The same basic operation is necessary for all other school and district and central office personnel. If work is not done, then incumbents should be released.

In addition, we should consider linking improvement in the basic skills of Chicago students to teacher compensation. When the next union contract is signed, wage increases should be directly tied to improvements in the basic skills of students. This concept should apply to everyone in the school system, including maintenance engineers, administrators, and teachers. Under such a system, a 10 percent improvement in test scores would yield a certain raise, and no raise, or even a salary decrease, would occur if test scores fall below a certain target. By making teachers accountable and rewarding them for improved student performance, authority and responsibility will be properly aligned. Finally, the business community should take the lead in this case. It is in our long-term best interest to support the schools and learning.

ASISH SEN is a member of the Chicago Board of Education.

JACQUELINE B. VAUGHN is president of the Chicago Teachers Union.

THOMAS FLANAGAN is managing partner of Deloitte & Touche, a "Big Six" accounting and consulting firm in Chicago.

This chapter examines achievement, attendance, and other indicators of quality education.

Reform and the Quality of Education in Chicago

Richard P. Niemiec, Herbert J. Walberg

Embodied in Chicago school reform is a very democratic ideal. It is the democracy of shared responsibility that makes, in part, the reform experiment so attractive and uniquely American. In a modern republic, instances of participatory decision making among the electorate are rare. It appears that no one wants reform to fail. It embodies too much of the ideal on which our government is based. Despite this appeal, it seems necessary to evaluate the results of the efforts thus far. We need to ask, Are the Chicago public schools (CPSs) better since reform legislation was passed? Is it working? To answer these questions, we need to address the intent of the legislation. In this, the Chicago School Reform Act of 1988 is clear:

> The General Assembly is committed to the belief that, while such urban schools should foster improvement and student growth in a number of areas, first priority should be given to achieving the following areas:
>
> 1. assuring that students achieve proficiency in reading, writing, mathematics and higher order thinking that equals or surpasses national norms;
> 2. assuring that students attend school regularly and graduate from high school at rates that equal or surpass national norms [P.A. 85-1418, Sec. 34-101].

The act calls for increased achievement, attendance, and graduation rates. How has Chicago fared in these areas since the enactment of the school reform act?

Table 9.1. Percentages of Students Scoring at or Above National Norms, 1989–1992

School Level	1989–1990	1990–1991	1991–1992
Elementary			
Reading	23.4	24.2	22.6
Mathematics	31.5	29.5	29.2
High School			
Reading	28.3	26.8	25.1
Mathematics	22.7	19.1	21.1

Student Achievement

Table 9.1 presents the results of standardized tests over the three years of reform for which data are available. The table lists the percentages of students scoring at or above national norms. In almost every instance, scores have declined. In a system as large as Chicago's, a loss of one percentage point translates into forty-one hundred students. Clearly, the reform effort has been unsuccessful in raising student achievement.

Student Attendance

Table 9.2 displays the attendance rates over the same three years of reform. The rates for elementary and high schools remained nearly the same across the three school years even though the Chicago Board of Education fired approximately five hundred of their truant officers in September 1992.

Graduation and Dropout Rates

Have graduation rates increased under reform? No. In fact, they have declined. In June 1989, 1990, and 1991, the reported graduation rates were 47.0 percent, 47.4 percent, and 43.7 percent, respectively. These figures compare with graduation rates all above 50 percent in the three years preceding reform. During the reform years, the annual reported dropout rate remained steady at 13.2 percent. In other words, in every year since local school councils (LSCs) were put in charge of the schools, almost fifty-five thousand students have dropped out.

Comparing Chicago with Other Cities

In addition to examining changes in the CPSs over time, we can compare CPS statistics with those from other big city school systems. In the fall of 1992, the Council of Great City Schools collected baseline data from its member school districts. Of the forty-seven largest school districts in the nation, Chicago ranked last in achievement and very near the bottom in

Table 9.2. Percentage Attendance Rates, 1989–1992

School Level	1989–1990	1990–1991	1991–1992
Elementary	92.6	92.5	92.6
High School	81.4	81.2	81.7

attendance and in graduation rates of the largest cities across the nation (Council of Great City Schools, 1992).

Local School Board Members' Reaction

These data, in themselves, would be less alarming if there was a sufficient indication that those with the power to change CPSs were taking adequate steps to ensure progress. In major surveys of LSC members (Mueller, Machiafava, and Baughn, 1991; Mueller, 1992), however, respondents indicated satisfaction with school progress. In 1991, 68 percent of LSC members thought the schools did better from the year before. They gave themselves an effectiveness rating of 4.0 (on a 5-point scale). By comparison, central office personnel were rated 2.8.

In discussing the results of the second-year survey, Mueller (1992, p. 13) wrote, "Survey results show that council members reported positive change and improvements in staff and student performance." All of this while tests scores fell, and more children left school for good.

Conclusion

How has Chicago reform fared? The data are mixed, the evaluation ambiguous. Obviously, the school reform act was passed, and the LSCs were fairly elected and, subsequently, reelected. They engaged in meetings, hired principals, completed school improvement plans, and engaged in other activities in accordance with the act. Even more, like LSCs, which included principals and elected parents, teachers, and community members, gave themselves good grades for their efforts and progress.

On the other hand, the central office seemed as expensive and refractory as ever. Power and money remained with a remote board and bureaucrats far from school sites. Worst, however, was that despite good intentions, the original goals were unattained. Test scores and attendance stayed low, dropout rates stayed high. Three years into the five-year trial period, the majority of these indicators point in the wrong direction.

The evaluation, of course, remains incomplete: Perhaps more time will show the ultimate benefits of the extraordinary reform act. But even more important, the intended beneficiaries—students, citizens, the business community, and great numbers of parents and community members not on LSCs—had little opportunity to make their views about reform known.

Policy changes, however, may not await more definitive evaluations. The middle-class and business exodus from the city continued apace. In late 1992, General Superintendent Ted Kimbrough announced his resignation before completing a brief term of office. In January 1993, the board opted to buy out the remainder of his contract. Supported by prominent academics, Mayor Richard Daley called for vouchers. Downstate legislators spoke again about breaking the CPS System into many smaller, more manageable free-standing school districts. CPSs faced a new, tough, state-wide accountability plan that would put on probation and eventually abolish schools that fail to improve outcomes. In 1993, the tide of events seemed ready to eclipse both the reform plan and its evaluation.

References

Council of Great City Schools. *National Urban Education Goals: Baseline Indicators, 1990–91.* Washington, D.C.: Council of Great City Schools, 1992.

Mueller, S. *1992 Survey of Local School Council Members: A Report of Findings.* Chicago: Chicago Board of Education, 1992.

Mueller, S., Marchiafava, B., and Baughn, G. *1991 Survey of Local School Council Members: A Report of Findings.* Chicago: Chicago Board of Education, 1991.

RICHARD P. NIEMIEC *teaches in the Chicago public schools.*

HERBERT J. WALBERG *is research professor of education at the University of Illinois at Chicago.*

INDEX

Academic performance: and business climate, 100; and Chicago Algebra Project, 89–90; and Coalition of Essential Schools, 83–84; and curriculum improvement, 81; 1982, scores, 1; and Paideia Program, 86–87; reform and, 7, 48–49, 96, 104; and teacher accountability, 100–101

Academy of Our Lady (case example), 70–71

Accountability: and local school councils, 7; and school improvement planning, 49–53; and special education, 68; teacher, 100–101

Adler, M. J., 84, 85

American College Test (ACT), 1, 83

Areson, J. C., 25

Baizerman, M., 25

Barber, B. B., 14

Bartot, V., 17, 18, 25

Baughn, G., 105

Bennett, A. L., 25, 29

Biklen, D., 57

Bryk, A. S., 10, 17, 30, 33, 43, 44, 46

Bucuvalas, M. J., 16

Business, and school reform, 100–101

Change: and choice strategy, 77; planned, 78; resistance to, 8–9; and school improvement, 78; teachers and instructional, 34–35; teaching/learning, 97–98

Chicago Algebra Project (CAP): costs, 92; evaluation, 89–91; implementation, 89; origin/philosophy, 88; prereform problems, 91–92; restructuring, 92; teaching/learning process, 88–89

Chicago Board of Education (CBE), 8, 10, 57, 59, 60, 67, 100

Chicago High School for the Agricultural Sciences (case example), 75–77

Chicago Panel on Public School Policy and Finance, 29, 43; case studies of schools, 49–53; midway report, 46–49

Chicago Public School (CPS) System: Algebra Project, 88–91; American College Test scores, 1; and budget deficit, 9; bureaucratic nature, 1, 8; Coalition of Essential Schools, 82–84; Home and Hospital programs, 91–92; 1982 academic achievement scores, 1; and other city school systems, 104–105; Paideia Program, 84–88; prereform special education problems, 58–60; quality/working conditions, 33–34; Secretary of Education 1987 report, 1; special education reform, 60–68; teachers' attitude toward, 33–35

Chicago School Reform Act of 1988: and Chicago Panel on Public School Policy and Finance, 43; intent, 103; mandates, 5; origin, 2; political background, 6; power realignment, 14, 81; and resource allocation, 95–96; and special education, 60, 62

Chicago school reform. *See* School reform

Chicago Teachers Union Quest Center, 99

Chicago Teachers Union, 9, 10, 24–25, 26, 29, 31, 35, 96, 98, 99

Choice programs, 73–77

Chubb, J., 69

Cibulka, J. G., 78

Cities-in-Schools program, 17

Coalition of Essential Schools (CES): and academic performance/dropout rate, 83–84; distribution, 83; evaluation, 83–84; less-is-more concept, 82–83; origin, 82; principles, 82; students, 83; and teaching/learning, 82

Coleman, J. S., 17, 18, 25, 69

Comer, J., 62

Community, and school reform, 10, 38, 96

Compton, D., 25

Consortium on Chicago School Research: and Chicago Panel on Public School Policy and Finance, 43–44; composition, 13; Conditions of Education reports, 22–23; elementary teacher/principal surveys, 29–40; implementation, 23–24; major activities, 24–25; purposes, 13; reporting

ORDERING INFORMATION

NEW DIRECTIONS FOR PROGRAM EVALUATION is a series of paperback books that presents the latest techniques and procedures for conducting useful evaluation studies of all types of programs. Books in the series are published quarterly in Spring, Summer, Fall, and Winter and are available for purchase by subscription and individually.

SUBSCRIPTIONS for 1993 cost $54.00 for individuals (a savings of 34 percent over single-copy prices) and $75.00 for institutions, agencies, and libraries. Please do not send institutional checks for personal subscriptions. Standing orders are accepted.

SINGLE COPIES cost $17.95 when payment accompanies order. (California, New Jersey, New York, and Washington, D.C., residents please include appropriate sales tax.) Billed orders will be charged postage and handling.

DISCOUNTS for quantity orders are available. Please write to the address below for information.

ALL ORDERS must include either the name of an individual or an official purchase order number. Please submit your order as follows:
    Subscriptions: specify series and year subscription is to begin
    Single copies: include individual title code (such as PE1)

MAIL ALL ORDERS TO:
    Jossey-Bass Publishers
    350 Sansome Street
    San Francisco, California 94104

FOR SINGLE-COPY SALES OUTSIDE OF THE UNITED STATES CONTACT:
    Maxwell Macmillan International Publishing Group
    866 Third Avenue
    New York, New York 10022

FOR SUBSCRIPTION SALES OUTSIDE OF THE UNITED STATES, contact any international subscription agency or Jossey-Bass directly.